MARSUPIALS and POLITICS

CONTEMPORARY
AUSTRALIAN PLAYS: 10

Barry Oakley

MARSUPIALS and POLITICS

Two Comedies

University of Queensland Press

St Lucia·London·New York

Published by
University of Queensland Press, St Lucia, Queensland, 1981
©Barry Oakley, 1981

Typeset by Press Etching Pty Ltd
Printed and bound by Hedges & Bell Pty Ltd, Melbourne

Distributed in the United Kingdom, Europe, the Middle East,
Africa, and the Caribbean by Prentice-Hall International,
International Book Distributors Ltd, 66 Wood Lane End, Hemel
Hempstead, Herts., England.

Published with the assistance of the Literature Board of the
Australia Council

*National Library of Australia
Cataloguing-in-Publication data*

Oakley, Barry, 1931-
  Marsupials and politics.

(Contemporary Australian plays; 10 ISSN 0589-7468).
ISBN 0 7022 1608 9.
ISBN 0 7022 1609 7 (pbk.).

I. Title (Series).

A822'.3

Contents

Also by Barry Oakley

Novels
A Wild Ass of a Man
A Salute to the Great McCarthy
Let's Hear It For Prendergast

Plays
The Feet of Daniel Mannix
Beware of Imitations
Bedfellows
A Lesson In English
The Ship's Whistle
The Great God Mogadon and Other Plays

Short Stories
Walking Through Tigerland

For Children
How They Caught Kevin Farrelly

Introduction

No other playwright of the past fifteen years has been more popular or more consistent in quality than Barry Oakley.

That he hasn't become a yardstick of commercial success, a ledger of bankability, as David Williamson has, is not Oakley's fault. In fact, one of the enduring annoyances of the "renaissance", is that credit, in both senses of the word, hasn't been given where it is due, to writers such as Oakley, not to mention an unsung collection of actors, directors and other writers.

It was Oakley's *The Feet of Daniel Mannix's* somewhat unexpected success that enables the Australian Performing Group to crawl out of a deep financial bog in 1971, by forcing a reluctant Australian Council for the Arts (as it then was) to see the permanence of the revolution. And his subsequent biennial contributions have always been reliably full, from *Bedfellows* to *Scanlan*.

However, none of Oakley's work has ever taken off into the commercial stratosphere — no *Club* nor *B. Franklin*. Maybe his work is too serious, too political for all out popularity. Maybe Oakley's time will come, when audiences grow in self confidence again. Popularity, of course, is only a limited measure of success. It might be that it is better seen as a measure of the success of a community, or of a fashion.

Theatre in any culture can't exist in an audienceless vacuum, and Oakley has been remarkably successful in talking to a substantial and important section of the community.

An early work like *Mannix* enabled, like all the best theatre of the early seventies, an audience to talk about religion, and politics, and culture without seeming to be nutcases, without having to do it directly. Audiences could talk about sensitive issues, things close to their view of themselves, by displacing the conversation onto the theatre. They weren't really talking about their feelings for the legendary Archbishop or the DLP or John Wren, they were talking about a play. And everyone knows that's a different scale of emotions, not threatening. The shared experience of the audience is still "out there", separate.

That was the closest the theatre at that time ever got to the "community", a special community, which used the theatre. Politics wasn't so much in the agitprop material, but, perversely, in the plays that dealt, however peripherally, with "realist" cultural/political issues dredged up during those heady times. It was the "realists" who were popular with the audience, who gave that gaggle of talkers some excuse, for example, to do a daring thing inside the polling booth.

They could, some of them, vote for the ALP, not to change Australia, but because Australia had changed, not because politics and urban renewal and medibank were subjects of conversation, but because the language and subjects of conversation, had become iconoclastic — sanctioned by the new culture.

We could talk about that poor blubbering dodo in *Beware of Imitations,* and suddenly the Menzies burden became lighter, less important. We could watch what happened to Billy Big Ears when he told lies (in the APG Revue of 1972) and know there was a feeling that something was growing. With hindsight however, whilst we were laughing, we should have been crying. It was all talk.

Like Frank, the "hero" of *Marsupials.*

Frank, like anyone who believes in staying in Australia when he knows all about it, is a person of paradox and contradiction. When events in his life — his wife's invitation to a successful expatriate journalist and old lover doing a piece on the antipodes for his London paper, the wife's decision to try her luck in that metropolis — cause him to reflect and rant on this country *and* decide to stay here, he uses all the arguments, knowing them to be mutually antithetical.

Australia's a horrible, anti-intellectual backwater, but it's also full of pretty good writers. It's got no culture, but it's got it's own style. And so on.

In Frank's case, the decision to stay in Australia apparently results in a major breakdown . . . the audience, however, has to live here.

Frank, like many of us, isn't good at relationships, isn't good at coping, and isn't very articulate (in spite of his educated veneer) about what he wants. He's never gotten over the affair his wife had with Tom before she married him. It still festers. He can't grapple seriously with the idea of his wife having an ambition stronger than her life with him.

He doesn't like success in expatriates who have left the sinking ship, and come back to pass comment. He doesn't like being in the zoo, but can't really explain his feelings to the visitors. Unemployment robs him of his voice, especially as he was sacked by a Pom.

Frank believes you have to live here to fully comprehend the incredible, unspeakable complexity of Australian society. And, finally, he believes that we shouldn't have to explain ourselves, here on the edge of the world, to visitors from the centre. We are independent.

His inability, in the end, to be able to encompass all these contradictionns in his life, and in his culture, cause him to autodestruct, implode.

The final image of the play is infinitely sad: A handshake in passing — mateship, European culture, all gone. Australia, the Australia Frank belongs to, "left behind, happily hedonistic, while an impotent intelligensia watches, drunk."

That's a black vision of Australia, and however much it's leavened by humour, it remains a bit grim for the carriage trade. Chaos though, and the troubles we have in reaching the millenium, are at the centre of nearly all Oakley's plays and novels. Like all good comic writing, his has destruction, violence and chaos close to its heart.

When he turns to farce, it's still there.

Politics, with its buffoonery and comic exaggeration and physical excess has more than a touch of Orton and Stoppard in its use of comic conventions and language to a serious purpose.

But here again, Australia doesn't fare well.

The antics of George Porter in his rise to, and fall from, the prime ministership are not only funny, they're true. Like Pere Ubu, George Porter is an essence of political truth.

There's Erwin, the German valet given to quoting (aptly) Nietsche — like a Shakespearean Fool. When you think about it, there's a little parody here and there of Macbeth, and Lear . . .

Not to mention Barbara, George's wife, the ambitious health food addict and Tai Chi exponent. And Black Jack McConnell, and a jogging LBJ-like U.S. President, and a conniving U.S. ambassador, and a desireable P.M.'s secretary, and the none too cunning visitor for Mujik, a vassal of the Soviet Union.

They're all there, they're all reiminiscent of people we've known, and loved and hated.

Having a ball . . .

Oakley, like most contemporary playwrights, feels free to adopt the forms, conventions, and languages of any kind of play that's ever been.

In *Politics,* physical gags run riot: physicalization of gags, might be a better way of putting it. There's a lot of the music hall vaudeville in this: changing clothes, sports action used as a metaphor, George's problem with the muesli diet, the use of Erwin as a buffer state, cameras in cufflinks. All these rough theatre devices have an honourable tradition in the Australian theatre since *Marvellous Melbourne, O'Malley* and *Mannix.* They are all part of the didactic side of comedy, in Oakley's search for action in the theatre — a search for ways to physicalize images to add to the humourous potential of talk. A farce, in short.

Oakley's language is funny, not because it makes use of the vernacular, though he invents some of his own to good effect from time to time, but because of its use of alliterative punning, the piling of exaggeration on exaggeration, mishearing of pronunciation, making a joke of a word by taking its meaning as it sounds or as it's spelled and inverting it, by taking seriously the meaning of a common phrase on the face of its words rather than what its vernacular meaning is . . . in short the use of a whole gamut of literary and aural devices in the theatre. With a whimsical rather than brutal effect.

Hardly anyone swears in an Oakley play. Oakley characters comment, develop, have conversations — they don't just trade insults in Orstralian. He takes the dangerous course of striving for the poetic.

In *Politics* the instrument is blunter, but essentially the same, aided by the immense variety of physical and sight gags in the play.

Max Gillies says that the biggest laugh to *Marsupials,*

however, was a "shock of recognition" . . . rather than the complete joke.

Sue and Frank wonder whether Tom's arrived yet:

FRANK: Maybe he's held up at the Fruit Fly Inspection Desk. [*big laugh*] They're trying to get the plum out of his mouth. [*little laugh*].

If laughter is the best medicine, then the body politic ought to be getting a bit better for these two plays.

However pessimistic they might be about our present condition, they can't help but raise our spirits, for they are intelligent, civilized works of a comic writer in command of his material, making us uncomfortable while we laugh.

GARRIE HUTCHINSON

Marsupials

CHARACTERS AND ORIGINAL CAST

Marsupials was first performed by the Melbourne Theatre Company in September 1979, directed by Bruce Myles. Cast were:

FRANK: **Max Gillies**
SUE: **Carol Burns**
TOM: **Sean Scully**
ESTATE AGENT: **Matthew King**

CHARACTERS

FRANK   A publisher's editor in his late thirties
SUE   A freelance journalist. Wife of Frank
TOM   A journalist. Late thirties
ESTATE AGENT   Thirties

Before each scene, if possible, the actors involved should be seen behind the set, waiting to enter, so that the realistic illusion is broken down. The set should be as abstract and spare as possible — although books, pictures and records are required. Imitation living room should be avoided.

SCENE 1

FRANK *and* SUE *enter together, almost with a suggestion of ritual procession. They sit and begin reading, he opening a paper, she an aerogram. After a silence, he registers the fact that it is an air-letter she's reading, and therefore slightly out of the ordinary.*

FRANK : Who is it?

SUE : [*Still reading.*] Tom.

FRANK : [*deliberately offhand, the name* TOM *obviously having implications.*] Uh huh. [*He returns to his paper, but curiosity soon gets the better of him.*] What's he want?

SUE : He's coming over.

FRANK : [*Again returning to his paper but obviously keen to know more.*] Business or pleasure?

SUE : Doing a couple of pieces on us. For *The Observer.*

FRANK : Flemington Racecourse, Australian Rules Football, Chiko Rolls, Bondi Beach and Ockers in blue singlets in the public bar. Whenever the English come out here, they can't get to the booze and beach quick enough. They're convinced the place is barbarous, so they go straight to the barbarians to prove it.

SUE : Tom is hardly English.

FRANK : What — after — twelve years in London? He's more English than they are.

SUE : He wants to stay with us while he's in Melbourne.

FRANK : [*Reading.*] "Since I'll be living out of suitcases most of the time, I was wondering if I could prevail upon your hospitality while in Melbourne." Well put. He *would* be prevailing.

SUE : He was kind enough to us while we were in London.

FRANK: Yeah. Kind. Made us feel like village simpletons. Dave and Mabel, sucking straws and staring up at Big Ben.

SUE: He was right — you mistook Trafalgar Square for Piccadilly Circus.

FRANK: [*Reading.*] "I'll be out there for four or five weeks"— what does he mean, *out*?

SUE: *Out.* They're at the hub, we're at the circumference.

FRANK: And the world's a wheel then, is it?

SUE: The world's made up of spheres. Spheres of influence. London's in the middle of one, New York's in the middle of another, and we're sort of — in between . . . in some kind of frontier where women don't go into the public bar.

FRANK: Frontier is it? Maybe that's why he wants to stay with us. For protection. So he won't be attacked by natives . . . we didn't stay at *his* place when we were over there.

SUE: In that doll's house in Islington? How could we?

FRANK: We weren't *asked*, that's the point. Not that I would have accepted . . . imagine living with Hilary . . . like a motorized dummy from a Harrod's window . . . if surgeons cut that woman open, she'd be tweed right through to the bone . . . how could he possibly have married her? Don't answer that.

SUE: Why shouldn't I answer it?

FRANK: It may prove embarrassing.

SUE: Not at all.

FRANK: He married her on the rebound.

SUE: Okay, okay—

FRANK: When did I last mention it?

SUE: You don't *have* to mention it. It's just *there*, all the time, underneath.

FRANK: He must have married her on the rebound, there's no other explanation . . . imagine living with that voice! Like the top of a can of beans — thin, sharp and tinny . . . And the forks! The *foie gras* from Fortnums! The formality!

SUE: Those tiny little rooms stuffed with antiques!

FRANK: She's imprisoned the guy in Liberty florals. It's on the couches, it's on the cushions, it's on the lavatory walls—

SUE: Slow poisoning with Goddard's Improved Silver Dip and Propert's Genuine Leather Polish.

FRANK: She polishes him with it too.

SUE: They live in genteel poverty all the week so they can entertain in style at the end of it.

FRANK : That's why he wants to stay with us. So he can pocket his accommodation allowance for a week.

SUE : He wants to see us again.

FRANK : He wants to see you again.

SUE : If he thinks of other women, it's because his own is too terrible to contemplate . . . I don't think he's game enough to divorce her . . . bad form and all that.

FRANK : Divorce her? And marry whom?

SUE : I'm only suggesting he escape . . . not walk through the prison gates again.

FRANK : It's like that is it? [*No answer.*] Yes, I suppose it is like that.

SUE : Divorce her — and marry whom — what did you mean by that?

FRANK : I meant, well . . . I don't know what I meant.

SUE : *I* know what you meant. You're still seething and fermenting after all these years.

FRANK : I was commenting, not fermenting.

SUE : Okay then, let him stay for a few days. Out of common politeness to an old friend.

FRANK : An old friend, by definition, is someone you don't have to worry about being polite to. I'd rather he didn't. Once was enough.

SUE : Haven't you had enough mileage out of that? Haven't I paid for that misdemeanour in full?

FRANK : You call having an affair with another man only eighteen months after we were married a misdemeanour?

SUE : After all these years? It's a pimple, a speck on the horizon.

FRANK : Well, it's still close to me.

[*Silence.*]

SUE : You *are* fermenting; I can hear you hissing and bubbling.

FRANK : When did I last mention it? When?

SUE : You don't *have* to mention it. You wear it. You carry it round with you. It's part of you and you don't know it. You have a kind of permanently aggrieved manner. As if I've done you a mortal injury. You've turned the chip on your shoulder into a military decoration — an epaulette.

FRANK : It's buried! Finished!

SUE : You said it was *close* to you a minute ago. Make up your mind.

FRANK: It *is* close to me. The shock of it's still in here, a psychic wound—
SUE: Right . . . right . . . okay . . . okay—
FRANK: — but I've — adjusted. I don't bear a grudge any more. I *understand* why you did it. That's how I've buried it — by making myself understand why. And because I understand, I'd rather he didn't stay.
SUE: You *think* you understand.
FRANK: I understand that nothing's changed. Nothing had changed when we saw him in London two years back, and nothing's changed now. You looked at him in London the same way you looked at him years before — and if he comes here now, you'll do it again.
SUE: Everything's changed. He's married, he's on the way up in Fleet Street, and he's just paying the colonies a visit. And while he's here, I want you to be hospitable to him.
FRANK: So you want him to stay?
SUE: I want him to stay.
FRANK: Okay, okay . . . lower the drawbridge, open the doors and wheel the horse into the yard.
[Blackout.]

SCENE 2

SUE *enters a bedroom area, to one side, with a colourful quilt.* FRANK *enters behind her, quietly, and watches as she spreads it on the bed, smooths it out, tucks it in, unaware of his presence.*
FRANK: New?
SUE: Yes, new.
FRANK: Expensive?
SUE: I don't think so, no.
FRANK: How much?
SUE: Eighty dollars.
FRANK: Eighty dollars! For a bed he'll occupy for a few days?
SUE: When he's gone, we can use it.
FRANK: If we're still together when he's gone.
SUE: And why shouldn't we be?
FRANK: If I were him, coming into that room — you've painted over the damp by the window, you've taken the Picasso

from the living room — and now an eighty dollar bed-spread—

SUE : Yes, go on.

FRANK : I'd think it's not so much a room, more a set of signals.

SUE : He comes from a civilized environment, and that's what I'm trying to give him.

FRANK : It's not a room, it's a welcome.

SUE : It's an honest room then.

FRANK : Then nothing *has* changed — you admit it?

SUE : I still have some feeling for the man — like you no doubt have for Cathy.

FRANK : Cathy and I were never involved the way you were — or *are*. How would *you* feel if I was to invite Cathy to stay for a few days?

SUE : I get on quite well with Cathy.

FRANK : The fact that I got involved with Cathy didn't really bother you—that's why you get on well with her. The truth is, nothing really bothers you as far as I'm concerned. You obviously don't care that I'm about to lose my job for example, otherwise you wouldn't have spent that eighty dollars.

SUE : It's my money! I earned it belting out articles for magazines!

FRANK : We're going to need every cent we've got for the next few months, don't you realize that?

SUE : But you're going to get another job.

FRANK : I still *might* get another job.

SUE : Might? One of the sharpest publisher's editors in town? It's might now, is it?

FRANK : Don't blame me. Blame the English multi-national that's gobbled us up. They're not interested in Australian publishing, so they're not interested in me . . . try to understand. It's harder to get another job if I'm doing the asking — I'm going round cap in hand — interviews, lunches, promises, promises — it's driving me crazy — while all *you* can think about is an eighty dollar bedspread — if I *can't* get another job . . .

SUE : —then I'll have to get a full-time one as a journalist, won't I?

FRANK : —yes, and pigs might fly—

SUE : —male chauvinist pigs — quite often fly—

FRANK : —if I can't get another job, and you can't — and we fall behind in our mortgage payments—

SUE : —who's the one that keeps them going? Me! Tapping it out for the women's magazines!

FRANK : —it's not enough. When we're evicted into the street [*Wrenching quilt off bed and wrapping it round himself like a cloak.*] we're going to need this damned thing, not him! We're going to need this to huddle under.

SUE : Melodrama — pure melodrama.

FRANK : —when I come home at night to our little bit of footpath after playing my gumleaf all day to people in theatre queues, everything will be okay, because I'll have a beautiful eighty dollar quilt to huddle under, with water-proof tassells at the edges!

SUE : [*Quietly.*] If you can't get another job, then I will. I'm earning half your salary working my backside off as a free-lance as it is — as well as keeping the family together — cooking and cleaning up after you and Natalie. God knows why I bother.

FRANK : If he knows, let's ask him. God, why does she bother? Not a sound, you've got him stumped too.

SUE : And don't give me that stuff about multi-nationals. I know why you're losing your job — and why you can't get another one.

FRANK : God, why is he losing his job and why can't he get another one?

SUE : Maybe it's because you drink too much.

FRANK : I do drink. I'm good at drinking. I also happen to be good at publishing. As a matter of fact, to be good at publishing you have to be good at drinking.

SUE : You do do quite a lot of it.

FRANK : [*Quietly*] If I drink — it's not to get myself through the day, but to get myself through the night. Sometimes, when I'm home with you — when the two of us are sitting in the room reading, with Mozart singing away on the stereo, I feel — lonelier than if I were on my own — loneliness intensified, because it's the only thing we share — quintessential loneliness. If I drink, that's why I do it.

SUE : What about me? The loneliness *I've* felt.

FRANK : Well, come on, out with it. Say the unsayable. Why are you lonely?

SUE : Because ... I gave up more than you'll ever know, that's why.

FRANK : And that's why you'll never buy a new bedspread for *us* — why ours is that patched old purple thing we've had for years.

SUE : The purple's appropriate. It's what they cover up church statues with during Lent.

FRANK : Aha, I see your symbolism — after Lent comes Easter. When the King returns to claim his Kingdom.
[*With slightly manic, ironic theatricality, he bows towards the door.*]

[*Blackout.*]

SCENE 3

SUE *inspects a Breughel print, then unhooks it from the wall.*
FRANK *is holding another print, a Sidney Nolan, and is obviously running out of patience.*

FRANK : First we have the Breughel there and the Sidney Nolan *there* — then you change 'em round, take 'em out, bring 'em back—

SUE : It looks unbalanced! Without the Picasso it looks unbalanced!

FRANK : Get it out of his room! Give *us* back Pablo, and he can have Sid ... He'll be here any minute and you're still rearranging the props.
[SUE, *contemplating and rearranging the pictures, doesn't answer.*]

SUE : [*Eventually.*] Hold the Nolan over there for a minute.

FRANK : [*Holding it up over his head ... it shows Ned Kelly.*] Sorry Ned — we're going to hang you all over again ... [*No answer as she considers.*] Just because Tom's little doll's house looks like a museum, *we* don't have to make exhibitions of ourselves—

SUE : Bring me in the damned Picasso and belt up.

FRANK : [*Going to one side and suddenly noticing.*]

Hey, wait a minute — where did this little number come from? [*Picks up and examines small table.*]

SUE : It's okay — don't panic — I got it cheap.

FRANK : Looks it . . . the most occasional table I've ever seen. Puff of wind'd blow it over . . . See those little holes? Borers . . . at least that proves it's edible . . . we can tuck into it when we run out of food.

SUE : Come on — the Picasso! Hang it — and then hang yourself!

FRANK : [*Bringing it to her.*] I dipped out again today. If I miss out with Heinemann's tomorrow it looks like the dole queue.

SUE : [*Hanging it.*] One of the great talents in publishing . . . the number of dinner tables you've bored with your coups.

FRANK : There just aren't the jobs any more—

SUE : Come on, give us a hand — he'll be here in a minute.

FRANK : I hate visitors from England! That guy from London that fired me — a company assassin with clipped accent and overgrown moustache — he takes me to lunch, waits till the coffee and port, then out comes the pearl-handled revolver — [*Imitating him.*] — "Frank old chap — the long and short of it is we're going to have to abandon our Australian publishing programme, so I'm afraid we'll have to abandon you. Frank! Come back! I don't mean immediately". Walked out on the bastard there and then . . . intruders in the office and now another one at home! [*Dropping the print he's been holding.*] Bugger the Breughel!

SUE : Calm down, for Christ's sake!

FRANK : You're the one that's nervous. All this bloody window dressing!

SUE : I'm not nervous about him, I'm nervous about *you*. You were like a lamb in London, but here, on your own territory—

FRANK : [*Slightly manic.*] I'll be a lion! [*Roaring.*] Hi Tom! [*Snarling.*] Welcome to darkest South Yarra!

SUE : [*Finishing her arrangement.*] Just try to control yourself when he's here, that's all I ask . . . the decencies . . . the essential civilities — is that too much to expect?

FRANK : You're all keyed up, aren't you? Let's see — I know what we want. Some appropriate music. Some welcoming sounds . . . [*Checking his records.*] *1812 Overture?* A trifle grandiose. *Carmina Burana?* too carnal and erotic ... I know — [*Looking around at the pictures on the walls.*] — Moussorgsky ... [*Quieter.*] *Pictures at an Exhibition* ... [*Putting record on.*]

SUE : Jesus you exhaust me. Get me a gin and tonic.

FRANK : Patience, patience, he'll be here soon. Bit of a change from twelve years ago, when we took him in like a beggar off the streets. He was the nervous one in those days.

SUE : God, that chicken coop in Carnegie with the concrete backyard ... an Arts degree, a husband, a baby and a bungalow out in the sticks. From the tragedies of Shakespeare to nappy wash in two years.

FRANK : Whatever you had to put up with, teaching was worse. Straight out of university and straight into Richmond Tech ... Tom and me, our Education Diplomas freshly stamped upon us like cattle brands.

SUE : And because the mighty Tom had an honours degree, you resented him even then.

FRANK : Because the mighty Tom had an honours degree, he looked down on everybody from a great height — and then he fell from it. Three months at the chalkface with forty farting adolescents and he collapses in a heap. At least I worked my bond out before I escaped from Devil's Island ... but not the great Tom — should've had a tame shrink like he did.

SUE : Come on — if that wasn't a nervous breakdown nothing was. He couldn't cope with the job and his girlfriend had left him. He didn't have a support in the world. Is he going to turn up or isn't he?

FRANK : Pass up an opportunity like this? Course he'll turn up.

SUE : But you're hoping like hell he won't.

[*Pause. They drink. He muses.*]

FRANK : Diploma. What a silly word. Papiloma. Carcinoma. Like a disease. We went to that school suffering from advanced diploma. By God we learned fast. Talk about the class war.

SUE : You got out pretty smartly yourself for that matter. Weren't *you* lucky you knew somebody in publishing. Couldn't brush the chalk off your coat quickly enough.

FRANK : But I worked my bond out first. I stuck it out while I had to. I did my three years' hard labour.

SUE : And Tom didn't — somehow he's a coward, a weakling, because he keeled over and flaked out in the staffroom. *You* were the coward, because you didn't want to take him in.

FRANK : And I was right by God. Visions, valiums, migraines, that awful Indonesian cigarette smoke coming up from under his door. And all the time I thought he was falling apart he was getting it together with you.

SUE : If *you'd* have gone to him yourself when he needed help, the whole damned situation mightn't have arisen.

FRANK : The "situation". A lovely loose tarpaulin of a word to throw over a pair of lost lovers. Whatever you did to him, it was mighty good therapy — over to London, into Fleet Street, and he's never looked back. Until now. You phoned the airport? . . . Yes Frank, I phoned the airport.

SUE : It arrived on time.

FRANK : Maybe he's held up at the Fruit Fly Inspection Desk. They're trying to get the plum out of his mouth. [*He opens a can of beer, spilling some in the process.*]

SUE : [*Wiping it up.*] And you're trying to get as much booze as possible into yours. That's why you talk through your nose. The words have no other way to get out.

FRANK : I see. [*Deliberately spilling some more.*] Well, let's show him how we really live.

SUE : [*Again wiping.*] Cut it out!

FRANK : Jesus, this is ridiculous. Do you want me to sit or slump? What effect are you after, the casual or the contained?

SUE : [*Finally breaking, and throwing a cushion in the air in despair.*] Oh bugger it! What's the use!

FRANK : Whoopee! Let's go for the lived-in look!
[*He throws a cushion, stands up, kicks another one.*]
The old ocker image! [*Undoes his shirt, to reveal athletic singlet. Slumps in the chair, with beer in hand, cigarette hanging from his lip.*]
[*Knock on door.*]

SUE : Oh shit, I knew it. [*Making last effort to tidy up before heading for door.*]

FRANK : Don't go, you're not the footman. [*In slack-jawed ocker style.*] Come in cobber!
[SUE *exits to door. As* TOM *enters,* FRANK *moves to greet him.*]

TOM : Pictures at an Exhibition!

SUE : [*Gesturing to the walls.*] There's the pictures— [*Gesturing to* FRANK.]—and there's the exhibition.

FRANK : [*Ocker style.*] Ow yer going?

TOM : [*Ocker style.*] Put it there mate.

FRANK : Long time no see. Kept all the form guides for you.

TOM : And the Footy Records I hope.

FRANK : Crack a can!

TOM : Pie and sauce!

[*Mutual ritual barracking sequence from their past.*]

FRANK : Carn the magpies!

TOM : Give him a free kick you animal!

FRANK : He was off! He was off!

TOM : Couldn't get a kick in a stampede!

FRANK : If it'd been a pudden, it would have gone all over you!

TOM : Chewy on your boot, chewy on your boot!

FRANK : [*Giving in.*] Phew, I'm exhausted.

TOM : [*Signalling a goal with fingers or arms.*]
Six points to the visitors!

FRANK : No need to go on and on.

TOM : [*To* SUE.] He looks all slumped over.

SUE : The little Aussie bleeder bleeds easy.

FRANK : Finish! The Australian colloquial championships are now over!

TOM : Hey — you're grey.

FRANK : The footpaths are grey, the skies are grey, the Shrine is grey — it's our natural colour in Melbourne. Grey.

SUE : Melbourne is pink and brown. It's a man in a brown cardigan reading a sporting paper the same colour as his face.

TOM : That's good — I can use that.

FRANK : That's your Young and Jackson's nineteen-fifties man. There's a new generation now.

SUE : Yeah — son of ocker — and he's worse. A car salesman with a Denis Lillee moustache, a crimson body shirt, and a Chrysler Charger in the built-in garage of his hacienda. They build the garage into the house these days — so the six-cylinder pig can sleep with the family, like in the middle ages.

FRANK : Isn't it marvellous? If we can have our six-cylinder pig in South Yarra, why can't they have 'em out in Bulleen?

SUE : I'll drive it, I'll ride in it, but I'm damned if I'll sleep with it.

TOM : Two authentic little furry Australians — in their natural habitat! They've dropped their gumnuts, sharpened their claws, and now they're going to scratch each other to death.

SUE : [*Pouring drinks.*] To Mr Young and Mr Jackson.

TOM : That's one place I'd really like to see again — Young and Jackson's.

FRANK : Young and Jackson's is a frontier survival!

TOM : That's why I want to go there.

FRANK : [*To* SUE.] See what I mean? I can introduce him to writers, publishers, civilized people — and all he wants to do is go to Young and Jackson's.

TOM : I want to go to Young and Jackson's and I want to take the tram out to Mount Albert and I want to stand in the outer at Victoria Park and watch Collingwood play, with a pie in one hand and a can of Fosters in the other.

FRANK : All the refined Englishmen that come out here talk like that. You're supposed to test the stereotypes, not devour them whole like a Noon pie.

SUE : Find the right ones, that's what matters. Get the images right — like the front fence up the road, featuring koala, Captain Cook, convicts and Christ knows what — from the Aborigines to the 1956 Olympics in two million inlaid sea-shells. Epic history in concrete.

FRANK : That's not typical — it's grotesque!

SUE : It's typical *because* it's grotesque! The poor guy hasn't got a tradition, so he's invented his own in shells.

TOM : Wait on — we *do* have a tradition—

FRANK : Who's "we"?

TOM : The Australians. Us.

FRANK : [*Lifting up one of* TOM'S *eyelids.*] You *are* one, are you? Is that the Hume Highway along there, or the M-1? You are wearing an athletic singlet and support?

TOM : We do have a tradition and you're acting it out.

FRANK : What am I doing?

SUE : You're being aggressive. You've got the Australian flag sewn on your underpants.

FRANK : I'm sorry. I've erred. Infringed the proprieties. [*Bowing and tugging at his forelock.*] Welcome to the Antipodes, and allow me to take your luggage to your room. Leave out any boots or shoes you'd like polished. [*He moves to the side of the stage with the cases.*]

SCENE 4

TOM *enters, opens a newspaper and reads. He's dressed, ready to go out. Enter* FRANK *in dressing gown. He pauses, as if lost in memory, then begins a nostalgic imitation.*

FRANK : "Boys, prepare yourself for a piece of music for artillery and orchestra. A rousing piece of music. Celebrating the triumphs of Napoleon. I'll write that name on the blackboard."
[*Looks at* TOM.] Means nothing? Strikes no chord?
[TOM *looks blank.*] "Boys, this splendid overture was written by a Russian composer called Tchaikovsky. I'll write that name on the board."
[*He turns to an imaginary board, as if to write.*] . . . "Stand up the boy who threw that." [*Again looking at* TOM, *who continues blank.*] Come on, the old guy that taught at Richmond Tech. He'd announce the record, tell them how exciting it was, put it on, then fall asleep in front of the class.

TOM : Alf—

FRANK : Yes, yes. Alf who? Alf who?

TOM : Alf—

FRANK : Wilkinson! How could you forget? How could you forget anything about that purgatorial year?

TOM : Hellish year.

FRANK : Purgatory, not hell, because we both got out of it.

TOM : Hell — because it seemed like a bloody eternity . . . the way the kids booed us the first day back, when we went out to take morning assembly . . . the straps the headmaster issued us with, like armaments before the onset of battle . . . and which, to my cost, I was too embarrassed to use.

FRANK : You had to use the strap. The strap was essential. I first used it during a lesson on Wordsworth's "Tintern Abbey". Wordsworth was wrong about nature. Nature is an adolescent boy, not a daffodil.

TOM : I couldn't use the strap. The kids agreed with me. Within a week they'd cut it up into little bits the size of biscuits.

FRANK : Remember Vince Kellaway? He was the Harold Larwood of strapping.

TOM : Vince Kellaway was a barbarian. I don't want to hear about Vince Kellaway.

FRANK : When Vince Kellaway gave the strap, he'd go back half a dozen steps to give himself a run-up to his victim. He'd come pounding in and then whack! When Vince Kellaway opened his shoulders, teachers used to peep in from the corridor.

TOM : Stop saying Vince Kellaway! Especially first thing in the morning.

FRANK : Sorry, I got carried away — could I have some of my paper please? The back part! Might I remind you that there's a small group of Australians, admittedly becoming extinct, who don't immediately turn to the sporting pages?

TOM : Take the front, what's it matter? The whole bloody lot's written by sportswriters. Listen to this: "next week, Michael Guerard, the inventor of *cuisine minceur*, using little or no eggs, flour or butter, is opening his own shop". I ask you — have you ever tried opening your own shop using little or no eggs, flour or butter?

FRANK : Pedant!

TOM : I see. Well get this, in the business pages: "The first seeds of disaster for Melbourne as the financial heart came in the 1890s when the city's banking industry was badly scarred by the land bubble burst." Four metaphors mixed in a single sentence! You can't let copy through like that.

FRANK : Write a letter to the editor then.

TOM : *You* write a letter to the editor. You're the one that'll have to put up with it. Listen to this: "Hawthorn skipper Don Scott has just returned from a badly sprained ankle". How can you return from a badly sprained ankle? A sentence like that in a national paper!

FRANK : [*Grabbing paper, defeated.*] If it's giving you so much pain, let me read the damn thing.

TOM : [*Getting up.*] You're welcome.

FRANK : [*Reading*] Where is it today?

TOM : Two newspaper editors, one politician, a guy from the Tourist Commission, lunch with the mayor at the Naval and Military Club — then maybe the Shrine and Young and Jackson's — patriotism and alcohol.

FRANK : That headmaster you were talking about — the guy that gave out the straps — he died the other day. Methodist, wowser, whinger, autocrat — the man with a mind like a time-book and a dustcoat for a heart.

TOM : Listen — I don't want to remember him, or Kellaway, or the kids, or anything about that time — understand?

FRANK : He had the most appropriate name in the world. God looked down upon him, saw into the navy-blue serge of his psyche and gave him the perfect name — Dullard! Roy Dullard!

TOM : To hell with Dullard!

FRANK : [*Gesturing upwards*] That's probably just what's being organized for him right now. He's being kept in after school — for good! [*Seeing* TOM *lingering slightly impatiently in doorway.*]

I'm boring you.

TOM : You're irritating me.

FRANK : You don't want the past retrieved.

TOM : It wasn't a very happy time.

FRANK : For either of us.

[*Silence.* TOM *still poised awkwardly in doorway.*]

I'm sorry. You're embarrassed.

TOM : I'm not embarrassed.

FRANK : I'm being — Australian. Lapse in taste.

TOM : Don't be ridiculous.

FRANK : I'm mentioning the unmentionable — I've committed the ultimate English sin — infringing the decencies.

TOM : I have to go.

FRANK : What, at eight-fifteen? Surely the past is safe enough by now.

TOM : So I'd have hoped.

FRANK : — decontaminated — not radioactive any more—

TOM : For heaven's sake yes! But let's not go on and on! Let's just accept it!

FRANK : I'd have thought talking about it is a way of accepting it.

TOM : To recall it is to — revive —

FRANK : And you'd rather not.

TOM : No, I'd rather not.

FRANK : After what I went through with Sue after you left for London, I'm not even allowed the satisfaction of making you feel slightly uncomfortable at breakfast.

TOM : You weren't the only one that suffered.

FRANK : I'm sorry. Must have been agony for both of you.

TOM : I'm asking you not to go on about it. I'm asking for a little more — sensitivity.

FRANK : It's because I'm sensitive I *do* go on about it.

TOM : Sensitive about yourself but not about others.

FRANK : If I were to be crassly insensitive at the moment, I'd accuse you of hypocrisy for saying that.

TOM : Please do. Be boorish. Say your piece. And just to get rid of one of *your* pet stereotypes, I don't give a fuck about gentility — British or anyone else's.

FRANK : A few days ago, over an expensive lunch, I was painlessly, surgically removed from my job by a pin-striped and pin-headed gentleman from the City of London. He was beautifully dressed, beautifully mannered and spoken — but if you got hold of some forceps and prised back his stiff upper lip d'you know what you'd find? Dracula fangs.

TOM : Sorry as I am to hear about your job, I can't quite see the point of your story . . . yes I can . . . you're threatened . . . by a real Englishman at the office and an imitation one at home.

FRANK : You misunderstand me.

TOM : I don't think I do. How do I get to Flinders Street?

FRANK : Take the tram at the Chapel Street corner, but duck down as you pass the Botanical Gardens. The natives there aren't fully subdued. And watch your accent. Hearing refined tones unpleasing to them, local ockers have been known to drag innocent visitors from their conveyances and beat them with clubs.

TOM : I'll watch out for the Naval and Military—
[*He exits.*]

FRANK : [*After him.*] Avoid all fruit fly inspections—you could be searched.

TOM : [*Poking his head in again, still irritated, not wanting* FRANK *to have the last say.*] Bananas!

FRANK : No, no — plums. [*Pointing to his mouth.*] Spit out all stoned fruit before conversing.

TOM : The broad accent—and the narrow mind!

FRANK : [*After him for the last time.*] Moind—not mind!
TOM : How'd you loike a meat poie in the oie?
         [*They freeze. Lights slowly down.*]

SCENE 5

SUE *is typing.* FRANK *enters with a typescript.*

FRANK : Got a minute? Listen to this: [*Reading.*]
    "Melbourne is outwardly unprepossessing. She doesn't
    sprawl round a spectacular harbour as Sydney does, but
    sits, erect as a maiden aunt, by the banks of the Yarra — a
    river that springs crystalline from the nearby Dandenong
    Ranges and ends up muddied and rainbowed with pollut-
    ing oils as it flows past the city."
SUE : Don't tell me you wrote that.
FRANK : He did. Pinched it off his cheap, occasional table. Sounds
    like the borers are working their way into his copy.
SUE : You snoop!
FRANK : This is public prose.
SUE : It's private until it apears in print.
FRANK : Oh, I'm sorry. I'll put it back. You don't want to hear the
    bit where he tells us about the soul of the city.
SUE : I didn't know it had one.
FRANK : That's what he says.
SUE : Okay, let's have it.
FRANK : It's snooping.
SUE : Alright, snoop away! Get on with it.
FRANK : [*Reading.*] "Has Melbourne a soul, a heart? On my way
    through town this morning I saw a group of Japanese
    tourists in search of it, cameras at the ready, but photo-
    graphing nothing. 'Stop', I wanted to say to them. 'You're
    at the centre, the axis. Look north, and what do you see? A
    huge brewery, slaker of the national thirst. Now look south
    — at the end of St Kilda Road, see that enormous ziggurat?
    That's the Shrine of Remembrance. Shrine and brewery,
    patriotism and beer . . .' "
TOM : [*Entering.*] . . . Australia was built on them.
FRANK : I knew that would happen.

TOM : Go on, go on.

FRANK : [*Somewhat embarrassed.*] " 'The Australian soul . . . is nourished on Anzac and alcohol.' "

[SUE *claps quietly, also embarrassed.*]

TOM : Thanks. It wasn't quite ready for public performance.

SUE : Sorry. We've been snooping.

FRANK : No, *I've* been snooping. I went into your room to make sure your possessions weren't being eaten by borers, saw it on the table . . . and, well, snooped.

TOM : Snooping would be just having a quick read. You exposed it indecently.

FRANK : Sorry about that.

TOM : That's okay.

FRANK : It's not okay. It's unforgivable.

TOM : I forgive you then.

FRANK : Don't forgive me yet — I feel — another lapse coming on. I think it's a load of old cobblers.

SUE : And I think it's spot on.

TOM : [*To* FRANK.] And I think it's none of your damned business.

FRANK : Quite so. But aren't you out here to get the picture right?

SUE : He *is* getting it right. That's why you don't like it.

FRANK : After three or four days? How can you get anything right in that time?

TOM : I was born here. I don't have to go round searching for the Australian soul. I'm wearing it — I've got it in here.

FRANK : You've forgotten all you ever knew about the Australian soul.

TOM : *I* haven't forgotten, *you* have. Being Australian is a kind of painless disease — it doesn't start hurting until you leave the place. I always *knew* I suffered from isolation, but I didn't actually *feel* it till I got to London. Suddenly, twelve thousand miles away, I saw Australia for the first time: an enormous suburb stretching from Melbourne to Brisbane — a million backyards laid end to end — people walking and talking as if they've been lobotomized — an endless pub with pot-bellied guys in shorts propped in the doorways like fibreglass dummies — [*Running out of breath and steam.*]

FRANK : [*Going up to him and peering at him.*] I think you've been out in the sun too long.

TOM: [*Embarrassed by his own outburst.*] Sorry.

SUE: What? Because you've told the truth? Why d'you think I want to get out of the place? [*As she's talking* FRANK *starts singing "Come on aussie come on".*] When we were in London, whenever I got homesick — will you shut up? — I'd go to the little library in Australia House and look at the papers. Fraser, Whitlam, Hawke, Fraser, Whitlam, Hawke — quiet! — a tight little self-enclosed world spinning round and round its own navel — it used to make me feel giddy — like peering down a hole into a cave.

FRANK: [*Chanting, and rising as he does so.*] The Alf! The Roy! The Ern! The Les! [*Holding his can high.*] *The Norm!*

SUE : Go on, keep it up — crack a joke and a can!

FRANK : But that's all we've got left isn't it? A beer and a joke between mates? Anzac and alcohol. [*Hopping along.*] The one-legged soldiers are condemned to malt and hops.

TOM : Oh come on, there's more to it than that — no one's saying that's the whole damned picture.

FRANK: You want the other part of the picture? [*Picking up magazine from the table.*] There's the other part of the picture — the *Encounters* and *Times Literary Supplements* that were put out before you arrived — we drink wine, we listen to music, we work incessantly on our vowel sounds so they won't get too nasal — and we read the right magazines! You're amongst friends, civilized people, all is not lost! [*Looking at* SUE] Why do we want to impress the visiting Czar? Answer that—

SUE: I'll answer that! I'll answer!

FRANK: — answer that and you're really starting to say something about the Australian soul.

SUE : You haven't got a soul, you wouldn't know what one looked like. I put those magazines there because *I* wanted to read them.

FRANK : They're six months old, they'd been put away, and suddenly now they're out.

SUE : I've been working so damned hard at the typewriter I haven't had *time* to read them — now that the pressure's off a bit I put them out — to *read*, and for no other reason. [*Pause after all this emotion.*]

TOM : I'm going to bed.

SUE : No you're not. Never mind about the Anzacs or the boys in the bar [*Going over to* FRANK.] — peer in there at the little bits of rag and bone that pass for the Australian soul. This is it, trapped in a chair — the genuine educated barbarian article. First he tries putting you down, then he turns on me — what's the matter with him? Why does he do it?

TOM : Bedtime! Enough in-fighting for one day!

SUE : Not enough! He does it because there's only one real sin in Aussie eyes — wanting to leave, to get out. You've done it and I want to do it and that is the unforgivable sin. To want to leave the finest country in the world!

FRANK : Please! No more angst! [*Getting up, looking away and exclaiming theatrically.*] Look, they're chopping down the cherry orchard — o woe — to have to live in the provinces so far from Moscow — shall we play backgammon?

SUE : [*To* TOM.] See? Every time I get too close to the bone, a gag.

FRANK : [*Quietly.*] You know what's wrong with the place. He knows and I know. That's easy. [*Reaching down a handful of books.*] But this. This is hard. I published these people. I got them started. All over the country people are doing things, positive things — in politics, education, journalism, film, Christ knows what. All you can do is wring your hands and whinge over the booze and the barbecues.

TOM : It's a draw, okay? Let's call it a night. [*Exits.*]

FRANK : [*Pause.*] Leave by all means, but get the mix right first — understand what you're leaving.

SUE : No one said I was leaving. I said I'd *like* to leave, that's all.

FRANK : You want to leave and I know why you want to leave — and it ain't got nothing to do with the culture cobber — nothing at all.

[*Lights slowly down.*]

INTERVAL

SCENE 6

FRANK *and* SUE *sitting at the table, having an after dinner drink.*

FRANK : Good day?
SUE : Not bad.
FRANK : Chap from Collins didn't ring did he?
SUE : Couldn't say really.
FRANK : Out on a job?
SUE : Not exactly, no.
FRANK : But out. You were out.
SUE : Yes, I was out . . . I went out with Tom. To the old house in Carnegie. The verandah's been ripped off, the sunblinds hang in strips over the windows, the paint's peeled, the jacaranda's gone from the front garden . . .
FRANK : So what did you expect? It's a mean little wooden house in a mean little wooden suburb. We spent years in that Outer Mongolia and I never want to go back again. What's the point of going back? And why did you go back with him?
SUE : He wanted to see it again. Alf the butcher's still there smoking his Temple Bars . . . St Anthony's has an ugly new marble front built onto it . . . the man with the limp and withered arm still runs the delicatessen . . .
FRANK : Carnegie *is* a limp and withered arm. Koornang Road's the end of the world . . . Carnegie isn't middle class or working class or any damned class — but sort of suspended in between . . . Tom didn't want to recall the past with me. Said it was best forgotten. And yet the two of you drive five miles across town to retrieve it like a couple of grave robbers.
SUE : We were visiting the damned grave, not digging it up.
FRANK : And the coffin itself — intact?
SUE : Our bedroom, is that what you mean?
FRANK : His bedroom. The room where you nursed him through his "breakdown" while I was fighting for my life against forty kids at a time. The red room with the cheap lino and the crimson lampshade — is that still there?
SUE : It's gone — that's enough!
FRANK : — the shade that cast a radioactive glow over everything, the chair, the bed, the infra-red bodies lying together.

SUE : You're not going to make me feel guilty any more!

FRANK : [*Quietly.*] The room where you spent the happiest hours of your life.

SUE : I never said that!

FRANK : Once.

SUE : When?

FRANK : You let it slip once. That night you were stoned after that party at the Kirkpatricks . . . you loved him then and you love him now and I want him to go.

SUE : We can't just order him out — he's just arrived . . . Besides, he's trying to help us.

FRANK : He'd be helping us if he went.

SUE : He's trying to get me a full-time job.

FRANK : How can *he* get you a job, when *you've* tried all over town and all they want is the occasional article?

SUE : Who's talking about here?

FRANK : Ah! The mist disappears, everything is clear! He's trying to get you over there with him in London, the hub of the universe!

SUE : Not me. Us.

FRANK : He doesn't want us. He wants you.

SUE : Never mind about what *he* wants. *I* want a full-time job, and I want to live in London.

FRANK : And *I* want to stay here. And I'd prefer you to be in a different city from him.

SUE : He hasn't *found* anything yet — let's fight it out when we have to.

FRANK : There'll be no fight, because there'll be no point in fighting. He'll find you a job, and you'll go, and there's nothing I can do about it. The wooden horse opens! The soldiers sneak out into the dark!

[*Blackout.*]

SCENE 7

SUE *is at her typewriter. Enter* TOM.

TOM : He's interested, but he wants to see some of your copy.

SUE : *You've* seen my copy—
TOM : — there's no *problem* with your copy, I've told him that. But he won't take my word for it. Editors rarely do.
SUE : The *South London Times?* A little suburban throwaway? And he has to see my copy?
TOM : It's hardly little — it sells 150,000 copies twice a week. You'll have to airmail him something.
SUE : I can't wait that long. Telex him something from your office.
TOM : I can't use the telex as a mailbag.
SUE : You're telexing your stuff back to the *Observer*.
TOM : Hang on—
SUE : I *want* something to hang on *to*. I can't live in limbo for two weeks.
TOM : Okay, okay. You'll get *your* job, and if my editor finds out, I'll probably lose mine . . . I've lost [*Nod of the head.*] *him* anyway. No doubt *he* thinks it's all part of a plan.
SUE : Frank? You never had him to lose.
TOM : Surely, after all these years . . .
SUE : These things, according to Frank, never die. They're immortal.
TOM : Everything dies sooner or later.
SUE : Some things take longer to die than others. Resentment for example. Frank's been suffering from it quietly for years. It's like malaria. Now and again it flares up.
TOM : Like when I'm around.
SUE : Naturally.
TOM : So when you found out I was coming over, why did you write and ask me to stay with you? And write secretly?
SUE : I wanted to see you again.
TOM : But I'd have seen you anyway.
SUE : Only for a couple of hours in a restaurant. I wanted to see you up close. And as for the secrecy, if Frank had known I'd asked you to stay, that would have been the end of it.
TOM : But now he thinks I pushed my way in here — that it's all my doing.
SUE : It doesn't matter what he thinks. He's too far gone. Away out there, beyond reality.
TOM : It matters very much what he thinks, because he's made me the scapegoat. I can feel the aggression in there, building,

trying to get out. Thank Christ I've only got another forty-eight hours.

SUE : You've only had a few days of it. I've had fourteen years. I've done my best with Frank, and he's done his best with me, and it's no good. I know it and he knows it. He also knows I was in love with you in a way I've never really been in love with him.

TOM : You've said so?

SUE : You don't have to say so. He just knows. And — resents.

TOM : Then he's *not* away out there beyond reality. He has reason for his resentment. You're keeping it alive. By getting me in here, you're feeding it.

SUE : *Getting* you in here. You were forced into it?

TOM : If I'd have felt anything like that, I'd have refused the invitation.

SUE : What exactly *did* you feel, when you got my letter?

TOM : It's — hard to explain how I felt — or feel.

SUE : You're an explanation specialist. You're going to explain Australia to the readers of the *Observer*. Surely you can explain yourself to me.

TOM : I don't feel I have to explain myself to you. Why should I?

SUE : You just have by your high and mighty tone.

TOM : I'm sorry, but if there's any explaining to do, I feel I ought to do it to Frank.

SUE : Go on then. Explain yourself to Frank.

TOM : I won't explain myself to Frank, I just feel I ought to.

SUE : Nothing you say to Frank would make the slightest difference — because you've lost him and he's lost you ... he's also lost his job, his friends ... his daughter can't abide him, so there's only me. I'm not a wife, I'm a charitable organization.

TOM : And you're asking me to be one too.

SUE : I don't care what you are — faith, hope or charity — just get me this job — get me out of here!

SCENE 8

Lights slowly up on FRANK *and* SUE *facing each other.*

FRANK : I'm expected to uproot everything — house, friends, kid—

SUE : I'm not expecting, I'm *asking* — and it's not definite yet — wait, for God's sake, till we know.

FRANK : He telexed your article. He's pushing hard.

SUE : I pushed *him* — he didn't want to do it.

FRANK : So let's get it right — if this little man in South London says yes, you'll have just four weeks to get out of this house and over there — and in that time we have to sell our house, uproot our daughter, upset our aged parents, farewell our friends — and disappear!

SUE : By which time, if I miss out, you'll be on the dole.

FRANK : I'm looking around, but it takes time — and this guy's letting you know in thirty-six hours or something.

SUE : You've hardly a chance in hell of getting another publishing job — you said so yourself.

FRANK : And what's South London offering — eighty quid a week!

SUE : We'll invest the money from the house sale, and that'll pay the rent.

FRANK : We'll be on the breadline for the rest of our lives. We'll have to live on bangers and toad-in-the-hole for the next thirty years! We'll get the bloat! And the winters'll finish us off.

SUE : You're trying Sydney for jobs — what happens if you land one?

FRANK : I guess we go to Sydney.

SUE : We uproot, just like you say.

FRANK : I'd have a chance in Sydney. London's a new ball game — no contacts, no friends, no style, and a thousand unemployed publisher's editors queueing up for every job. It's crazy. I'm not doing it.

SUE : That's too bad then.

FRANK : Because you *are* going to do it, is that what you mean? No good telling me to wait, it's not definite yet, because if the man in Southwark says yes, then yes it is. Never mind about me . . . or Natalie.

SUE : Natalie would like to live in London.

FRANK : You've worked on her ever since we've got back. For two years you've brainwashed Natalie about getting out of the billabong and into the big world.

SUE : This is a billabong and London is the big world. She's not brainwashed — she knows and I know and we both want to go.

FRANK : She knows? At twelve? What about her ballet and music lessons?

SUE : Well, what about them? Who's going to pay for them here? Are you?

FRANK : What about the scholarship to Melton Hall next year? One of Melbourne's best schools.

SUE : It's a snob school — she can do without that school.

FRANK : Ah, we've changed on that one have we? Become all egalitarian now that we're moving in with the cloth caps and the smoked kippers.

SUE : I never wanted her to go to that school. You were the one because it saved you money.

FRANK : It's a waste of a good scholarship.

SUE : Come to think of it, you never cared about her ballet or music either. I've never heard you give a damn about anything to do with her future before — why the sudden worry now?

FRANK : Because now I have to worry. Have you forgotten the stories Josie Murphy told us about teaching in a South London comprehensive? The tough little tarts from Brixton with the spiky hair and the tattoos on their arms? They'll civilize Natalie all right. The first time Australia beats the Poms in a test match they'll roll her in the dunnies and stick her head down the bowl.

SUE : Don't try on me what you're trying on Natalie because it won't work. Trying to scare the life out of her — you're using her as a pawn to stop me from going.

FRANK : I'm her father and I don't want her to go. If she goes to school in South London, she'll end up behind a shop counter in Selfridge's.

SUE : If the school's no good I'll find her a better one.

FRANK : There'll be no finding on eighty quid a week. On that money, you'll get a council flat four feet wide with a rented TV in one corner and a coldwater tap in the other . . . and when you can save the price of a bus ticket, a game of bingo once a week. She's not going!

SUE : You can't stop her from going!

FRANK : I'll get a court order!

SUE : You're crazy! She prefers to be with me and I have a job to go to! Stop being a stick-in-the-mud. Leave the billabong and come over with us. See if the bunyip can adjust to the big world.

FRANK : And if it won't?

SUE : Then it's the ice age, or the drought, or whatever happened to bunyips.

FRANK : Nothing every happened to bunyips. They never existed.

SUE : And nothing's ever happened to you — for the same reason. Creatures that can't make decisions stay stuck in the mud.

FRANK : I made one decision, years ago, and look where that got me.

SUE : I made one too. But I'm not making another one like it. This time I do what *I* want. Not what you want or our mothers and fathers want or anyone else wants.

FRANK : Then it is goodbye then, isn't it.

SUE : It mightn't be — I might not get the job.

FRANK : Irrespective of whether you get the job, and irrespective of whether we go on cohabiting for a while, this is it then — you're saying goodbye to me, so I'll say it to you.
[*He starts to exit walking backwards in strange ritual fashion, waving.*]
... I'll be back for meals and sleeping accommodation — but this is hail and farewell ... after fourteen years together something mysterious happens to them ... and they drift away into the night.

[*Lights slowly down.*]

SCENE 9

Lights up on TOM, *ready to go, with two suitcases nearby.*
Enter SUE.

SUE : Arrogant pig. Made me sound like the tealady.

TOM : [*Impatiently.*] Yes, but did you get the job?

SUE : Yes, I got the job, but I don't like the sound of him.

TOM : Started off selling washing machines in the Old Kent Road.

SUE : Just what he sounds like — a discount salesman.

TOM : I'm sure you'll cope — congratulations.

SUE : I was rather hoping he'd say no ... if he'd have said no, it would have solved everything. I'd have to stay here and that would be that.

TOM : See you in London then.

SUE : — you know, I didn't really get on very well with Hilary.

TOM : Yes I know. Well, if *you* just come over—

SUE : Yes—

TOM : *We* won't see much of you, but I will.

SUE : Well, well. Down with the English reserve — unfurl the umbrella, and tear up the *Times*. Wasn't I given to understand that your feelings were complicated?

TOM : Wait a minute—

SUE : In fact, downright inexplicable.

TOM : Maybe seeing you over there will help sort them out.

SUE : If seeing me helps you, I'd rather you started sorting right now.

TOM : I can't do that in five minutes!

SUE : Come on — you're used to deadlines.

TOM : Well — you strip a man of everything — wife, daughter, house —

SUE : He's stripping himself. He can come with us if he wants to.

TOM : Just a minute — his friends, his pubs, his life — everything's here! You can't expect him to give all that up just so you can get to London.

SUE : If he got a job in London, I'd be expected to do all those things. Why is it so wrong just because *I've* got the job and not him? And as for this stripping you're talking about, I've done enough of that in the past. I stripped myself of you.

TOM : We stripped ourselves of each other. We had to do that. It's too late now ... we've got other commitments.

SUE : Commitments?

TOM : We have other obligations now!

SUE : Your marriage to Hilary is an obligation?

TOM : Hilary and I have our problems. Who doesn't? But that doesn't mean I want to leave her.

SUE : What does it mean then — I'm going to be a little bit of Australia on the side?

TOM : Good God!

SUE: Sorry to put it so crudely. Crudity is an Australian specialty. We're trying to get it put in the Olympic Games.

TOM: I meant — I'd see you without Hilary — but more as an old friend.

SUE: I'm not an old friend! Don't demean that relationship!

TOM: Okay, I meant more than friendship — I don't know what I bloody well meant — I think I meant I would enjoy your company. I'm even starting to doubt that. — I'd better go. [*Enter* FRANK *Pause.*]

FRANK: Why the gloom? Miss out on the job?

SUE: No I got it.

FRANK: Congratulations . . . [*To* TOM.] Happy?

TOM: Happy to be leaving town, yes . . . I know, it's all my fault.

FRANK: No, I was wrong, blaming you — it's what *she* wants. She's to blame. Which really means I am. I can't hold down a wife or a job. I'm bunyipped.

SUE: In other words you failed again today.

FRANK: Right. I ended up, after lunch, in the park. Sitting on a seat with my feet in the icy-pole wrappers. No place like a park for philosophy.

TOM: Well, I'm going.

FRANK: Of course. I mean this could get ugly. This fellow could transgress. His upper lip is impotent — refuses to stay stiff.

TOM: I'm tired of jokes about upper lips. Why don't you button up your lower one. [*Over to* SUE *to say goodbye.*] I'll be back from Sydney in a month to catch the plane home.

SUE: I'll miss you then. The washing machine salesman wants me there in three weeks.

FRANK: *I'll* still be here. You can pay me a visit and catch up with her in London.

TOM: Look, all it needs is for one of you to give in. *You* damn well go to London with her or *you* stay here with him. Someone give in! [*Silence.*] Okay, I'll be the mug. You do realize you won't be able to make much more over there than you're getting now as a freelance?

SUE: I want a regular job — not advice! I know what I'm in for — council housing scandals, old lady mugged in Peckham

Park, butcher puts too much sulphur dioxide in the sausages—

TOM : And is that worth giving it all up for?

SUE : Isn't it amazing? Bloody men!

TOM : [*Picking up luggage and storming out.*] I *feel* bloody! It's been spilt here for days!

[*Pause.*]

FRANK : [*Clapping genteelly.*] Splendid. Well done. All that of course was for my benefit. Very plausible it was too.

SUE : Let me tell you something for *your* benefit. Do you know why we've survived together for so long? Because there's never been enough passion to tear us apart — never have we come to the boil, never! We exist on compromises — we have a kind of treaty between us. I want more than that.

FRANK : So do I. Know which park I went to today? Treasury Gardens. Where I used to meet Cathy. I did a kind of pilgrimage. Around the sacred places. The fairy tree, Captain Cook's Cottage, the kiosk, the miniature English Village . . . And then I rang her up.

SUE : What did she say?

FRANK : She's moved. Gone. Living in Adelaide somewhere.

SUE : So what'll you do then?

FRANK : [*Suddenly.*] I know what I'll do. Let's have a party. A farewell party. I'll say farewell to you, and you'll say farewell to me, and our friends'll say farewell to both of us. [*Finger to temple.*] Let's go out with a bang.

[*Blackout.*]

SCENE 10

Enter FRANK, *hung over, a zombie in pyjamas. Enter* SUE, *also fragile. As they talk they wander about almost in slow motion, making token attempts to clean up.*

SUE : Never have I seen you so drunk. Never.

FRANK : I had reason.

SUE : So did I. The Thompsons went early.

FRANK : The Thompsons aren't party people any more. D'you

know what she said to me when I lit up a cigarette in front of her? Blow that towards me, she said, and it's assault. I laughed, I lit up and she lit off.

SUE : The Thompsons have given up booze, cigarettes, meat, sugar and television. They eat organic food that looks like gravel, they wear their own hand-knitted greasy-wool garments that make them look like upright sheep, and they get their kids up at gunpoint at six every morning to play Beethoven sonatas.

FRANK : Bloody puritans . . . I won't miss them.

SUE : You're definitely going to Sydney?

FRANK : Can't stay here, can I, if you're selling the house.

FRANK : If the invitation had sounded a bit more enthusiastic in the first place, I just might have. You don't really want me to go and I don't really want to go either.

SUE : Great time to be selling. Someone seems to have splashed claret over every flat surface. Bill and Jack stood in a corner all night arguing environmental conservation and covered the entire area with booze stains and cigarette butts . . .

FRANK : The more I said I was only going to Sydney for a while to rejoin you later in London, the less people believed me. Should have told them the truth.

SUE : Still not quite sure what exactly the truth is.

FRANK : You know what the truth is.

SUE : Ken and Margaret seemed to be getting on well together.

FRANK : I thought they were separated.

SUE : That's why they're getting on well together.

FRANK : Why didn't the Kirkpatricks come?

SUE : Because you insulted Ben at their last dinner party. He was going on and on about what a superb nose the wine had, so you tried to take it up through your nostrils.

FRANK : Like snuff.

SUE : Yes, like snuff. Who was the tough little guy with the safety pin in his ear that Norman was trying to get off with?

FRANK : Oh Christ, yes!

SUE : The more he abused Norman, the more Norman loved it.

FRANK : Norman's used to abusing himself.

SUE : The Hendersons left early too.

FRANK : That could have been my fault.

SUE : What did you do? It didn't have anything to do with his promotion by any chance?

FRANK : The bastard! He timed it perfectly. After I'd admitted I'd just lost *my* job, he casually let it slip that he'd just been made a director of Penguins. "Congratulations", I said, "What's it feel like, making the transfer from publishing to the zoo." I didn't see him after that.

SUE : Why not come over with us . . . try it just for a while.

FRANK : Because it won't work. Our marriage has been held together by the network around it. Once you cut that away — friends, in-laws — the inner web starts to collapse — the filaments start to go . . . Phew. I'm starting to go. You wouldn't have an Alka-Seltzer handy?

SUE : You'll have to get things for yourself from now on.

FRANK : Anyone who can get their own Alka-Seltzer doesn't need an Alka-Seltzer.

SUE : The food! The fags! The filth! As if all the meals and all the smokes and all the drinks we've had together have swollen up in a flash flood and covered the damn house! . . . Who was your gummy little friend with the pudding basin haircut who looked as if he'd slept in his clothes for the last six months?

FRANK : That was California Chris, a Carlton underground poet.

SUE : He looks it. Like one of those brushes you poke along pipes to clear blockages.

FRANK : Did you say gummy? I should warn you — he arrived with his dentures in.

SUE : That means they're still around here somewhere, waiting for us like beartraps.

FRANK : I think the only time he ever eats is when he goes to other people's parties. He wolfed down that entire plate of salmon mousse. He was still here at four o'clock in the morning. I trod on him on my way to the loo. Frightened the hell out of me! He leapt up at me and said "mmmm. m-mmmm. mmmm.", which I took to mean, "Fantastic party man, could you lend me ten dollars." — Open some windows.

SUE : Not till we clean up. The blowflies are queueing up out there.

FRANK : "The Reverend William Frisbee". What's this? . . . Oh, I know ... that crazy short story writer, what's his name, Michael somebody, who still thinks I'm the man to get him into print! Every time he gets into this place, he leaves behind a piece of fiction.

SUE : [*Picking up typescript.*] Listen to this ...

FRANK : Don't read it.

SUE : "The Reverend William Frisbee was a most unusual man. He was also very small, very short-sighted, and very deaf. And he had knobs on his face."

FRANK : It's all so bloody crazy ... The pretensions of these people. Our pretensions. Society can't survive without pretensions ... Excuse me ...

SUE : I want a hand.

FRANK : ... I think I'm going to throw up.
[*Stops and starts across the room as if fearful of getting the process going.*] Fourteen years of married life ... I started it on my knees in front of the high altar and I'm finishing it on my knees — heaving into the toilet bowl. [*He exits.*]

[*Lights slowly down.*]

SCENE 11

Empty stage. SUE'*s voice off.*

SUE : Taxi in five minutes!
[*Enter* SUE *agitated.*]
Think, think ... what have I left behind?
[*Enter* FRANK *with her suitcases.*]

FRANK : Don't answer that.

SUE : Too late now — you had your chance.

FRANK : [*Sitting on cases, as calm and abstracted as she is excited.*] If it were me, I'd go to Rome. I liked Rome.

SUE : You wrote a good travel piece about Rome ... open that case a sec — can't find the toilet bag—

FRANK : I'm planning a companion piece about Carnegie.

SUE : Rome was great. Except for the traffic. Swarms of little Fiats buzzing up and down the Corso.

FRANK : Remember that poor dog we saw cut in half by a car on the autostrada.

SUE : Yes, I remember.

FRANK : Remember what I said? The dog is Rome, the she-wolf. Torn apart by the motor car.

SUE : You should write more. Do a collection of travel pieces. Go for a grant.

FRANK : I'd start with Carnegie station. Where the undesirables used to loiter in the little reserve. I might join them. I'd be welcomed. I'd be big deal amongst the undesirables.

SUE : You had another good line. About those prostitutes we saw squatting by the Appian Way with their legs wide apart. Something about a notice they should have had on their laps. I know, this way to the Catacombs. You really should write more.

FRANK : I'd proceed down the lane, then over the railway line at that crossing where that Hungarian guy killed himself . . .

SUE : Frank . . .

FRANK : Turn right, past Koornang Road, and there, in the sixth weatherboard along, you'd find the Kennedys, Frank and Sue — Frank had left teaching and was on his way up in publishing. Sue was into Coonawarra Claret and Scandinavian furniture . . . Natalie was into nappies.

SUE : Come on. Come out and say goodbye to Natalie.

FRANK : I've said goodbye to Natalie . . . Remember when old Father Gleeson roared at us to take the baby out when he was preaching on the subject, suffer little children to come unto me?

SUE : Are you all right?

FRANK : Fine, fine . . . I liked Rome, I liked Paris, but something went wrong in London. You became preoccupied and tense in London. It was like going to bed with a bowstring. Strange things started to happen to me in London. The bridgework across my lower teeth collapsed. I twisted my ankle going into Westminster Abbey. We had that terrible meal with Tom in Soho. You hadn't seen each other for ten years — and the more you tried to ignore one another the more obvious it became. The pair of you were like negative and positive poles . . . I was stunned, pushed about by powerful magnetic forces . . . I felt — attenuated, a ghost, a shadow, a nothing — here were these two people who wanted desperately to be alone, and somehow, for no very clear reason, I was there, in the way...

SUE : [*With relief.*] The taxi! Help me with the cases!

FRANK : [*Determined to finish.*] In London I turned into a kind of nobody — I became obsessed with my passport, my traveller's cheques, my plane ticket, as if they were the only proof of my existence — I checked my pockets all the time as though if I lost them, I'd suddenly cease to exist.

SUE: You can't go on like this — you've built a paranoid wall round yourself — break out of it for God's sake and come on after us—

FRANK: I've got exactly the same sensation *now*, as if I'm being emptied out, all my pockets, everything — I don't *feel* anything, I don't *mind* your going, I'm drained, disembodied, floating—

SUE : Come over! Come back to earth! [*She gets the cases to the doorway.*]

FRANK : [*Suddenly noticing it.*] Natalie's guitar! You've forgotten Natalie's guitar!

SUE : She doesn't want it any more — it's falling apart!

FRANK : There's nothing wrong with this guitar! It's a perfectly good guitar!

SUE : She can't take it on the plane anyway! Bye!

[*They kiss.*]

FRANK : Bye.

[*She goes. He stands, preoccupied, holding the guitar.*]

[*Lights down.*]

SCENE 12

FRANK *has Beethoven's Consecration of the House overture on loudly. He conducts the music. Enter* ESTATE AGENT, *irate.*

AGENT: He's almost there! I've just about got you a sale out there! And you know what he likes most about the place? It's not the trees, it's not the courtyard, it's the peace and quiet! The peace and quiet he loves! And then boom! You almost blast him over the front fence! ... Listen, I've nearly got him, know what I mean? But he's worried about the foundations. Your foundations are not good.

FRANK : The foundations — and the fleas! Don't forget the fleas!

AGENT : The fleas?

FRANK : Your "For Sale" notice out on the fence — you left 'em out! Charming weatherboard home, period character, iron lace verandah, modern kitchen — and in summer, wall-to-wall fleas! Laid on! In every room!

AGENT : Don't yell it out.

FRANK : [*Yelling.*] The fleas! Mind your ankles!

AGENT : I've spent hours on this sale! I've worked my arse off for this sale!

FRANK : [*Ignoring him.*] You'll be okay — as long as you keep moving!

AGENT : He's gone. Bugger me, you've gone and blown it, you crazy fool!

FRANK : [*Turns music up and conducts.*] *Consecration of the House* Overture! You like Beethoven? You look more like a Mantovani man to me. Mantovani and his Singing Strings ... I'm purifying the place ... getting rid of the household gods!

AGENT : [*Turns it off.*] Hey — hey. I've got another fellow due right now — what's it to be — are we going to sell the property or aren't we?

FRANK : If you want to sell it, sell it — what's it to do with me?

AGENT : What's it to do with you? You're the owner, for Christ's sake. You hired us to do the job.

FRANK : I didn't hire you my friend. My wife did.

AGENT : I get it. She wants to, and you don't.

FRANK : Tell me. Why do you call yourselves real estate agents? Is there some doubt about your existence?

AGENT : Listen pal, I know, I can smell the stuff on your breath — if I light a match in here the whole place'll go up. Don't come the clever dick, okay? I don't enjoy doing this. It just happens to be my fucking job. What say you just fold up your tent, crawl into a cupboard, and let me get on with it?

FRANK : See that stain down there? One of our leading writers did that. Poured himself a claret, put the glass carefully down on the floor, then sat on it. Doctor needed a jeweller's eye-piece to get the glass out of his arse. This is a vintage house!

AGENT: It's a vintage house all right — you bet it is. Booze stains everywhere you look from arsehole to breakfast table. If I find a guy who's stone deaf, partially sighted and without his sense of smell, I'll have a chance to sell your charming little weatherboard terrace. Do you want me to sell it or don't you?

FRANK: Sell it — but don't forget the fleas — or the leak in the roof. Drips down there — right onto Henry Lawson. He's probably dying for a drink right now.

AGENT: Right! Here he comes ... okay now? Got your act together? I am going to go out and show this gentleman the many attractive features of this desirable residence. Okay? All quiet on the Western front? Not going to carve your name on the piano? Or crap on the carpet?

FRANK: I like my house! This is the only house I've ever lived in that I like! I worked my backside off to pay for this house!

AGENT: Your fucking house is a dirty house! You can have it if you want it — yes or no! I hate your bloody house!

FRANK: The place suits me — so sell it! Draw up the deeds! Heat up the sealing wax! Stick on the stamps! ... And tell them, when they buy it, just how lucky they are. They're getting a haunted house. Tell them not to worry if they hear any strange noises — it'll be me, bumping round up there in the ceiling ... my spirit will never leave this house ... the fleas down here — and me up there — you tell 'em!

AGENT: Yair, yair, I'll tell 'em, don't you worry. Just keep your powder dry, don't go near the stereo, and leave the rest to me — okay?

[AGENT *goes.* FRANK *goes to stereo, turns music on again. Light down on him conducting.*]

SCENE 13

Darkness. TOM's *voice*

TOM: Frank? Frank ...
[*Soft lamplight comes up, switched on by* TOM. *It reveals* FRANK *asleep on the floor, surrounded by cartons of books from the partly emptied shelves. Also a bottle or two.*]

TOM : [*Shaking him.*] Frank!

FRANK : [*Waking up suddenly.*] Jesus! . . . How'd *you* get in?

TOM : Through the window.

FRANK : Which window.

TOM : Your bedroom window.

FRANK : Perfect. I like that . . . Well, what's the problem?

TOM : There's no problem

FRANK : You wouldn't have called if there wasn't a problem. I'm the problem. The loose end. The floating participle. Looking for a nice noun to latch itself on to . . . [*Pouring a drink for himself.*] I know one — alcohol . . . Alcohol and I are engaged. I'm into alcohol — [*Drinking.*] and alcohol's into me.

[*Pause.*]

TOM : How's Sue?

FRANK : Sue's okay. You know as well as I do. She rang me yesterday. You'd rung her the day before . . . There's a glass round here somewhere.

[*Pause.*]

How was Sydney?

TOM : I enjoyed Sydney. Sydney was tranquillity itself. I stayed in a motel in Sydney.

[*Pause.*]

All this seems so unnecessary.

FRANK : Seems fated to me. Inexorable. Fixed. Predetermined. Had to happen.

TOM : All you need is a plane ticket. She *wants* you over there.

FRANK : You're the one she wants. I'm getting out of the way.

TOM : Frank, that's nonsense.

FRANK : [*Resuming packing the books.*] *Away* from the magnetic field, not back *into* it again.

TOM : Come back with me! Come on! You're packed, your house is sold—

FRANK : Know what the new owners said? They're going to put a pool down in the yard. Sounds like a rebellion or a pet animal.

TOM : Come on! I'm going in the morning!

FRANK : Go away! Leave me alone! I'm staying here! I belong here! You don't understand. You're going to London, and I'm going to Carnegie. To the centre for you, to the circumference for me! I'm going to take a train to Carnegie station, and walk along Koornang Road about ten o'clock one Sunday night — to the end of the world!

TOM : You're unreachable. You want out — and no one's going to stop you! You're — enjoying it!

FRANK : I don't want out! I'm forced out!

TOM : You're not forced out! It's up to you! Even now!

FRANK : Forces are spinning me out, centrifugal forces, powers, emotions! While you're flying — in! All we can do is hail one another from passing vehicles. Quickly, while we're passing — your hand!

[*They shake hands.*]

Politics
(A Farce)

CHARACTERS

HARRY SHANAHAN   Prime Minister of Australia (fifties)
GEORGE PORTER   His successor (fifties)
BARBARA PORTER   George's wife (forty)
MR PERCHA   Visitor from Mujik (forties)
ERWIN GRUBER   Porter's German aide (diminutive)
ELAINE   Secretary to both prime ministers
TELEVISION CAMERAMAN/DIRECTOR

FLOYD P. SUPPLE   US envoy to Australia
MR OMIRA   Prime Minister of Japan
PRESIDENT OF THE UNITED STATES
BLACK JACK McCONNELL   Influential politician
GRAND OLD MAN OF THE PARTY
SYNDROME   A psychiatrist
MR IAN CITIZEN
MRS NORMA CITIZEN
POLICEMAN

The play requires a cast of seven. With one exception (McCONNELL) the characters below the space appear once only — so with some doubling, a cast of five actors and two actresses is all that's needed.

SCENE I

The waiting area outside the office of the prime minister of Australia — the doors of which are upstage, impressive, emblazoned with a coat of arms.
Collage of parliamentary broadcasts, which reaches peak then fades as lights go up.
George Porter and Erwin, his aide, sit, waiting. Erwin is calm, absorbed in his book. Porter, impatient, obviously sick of waiting, gets up and starts pacing.

GEORGE : [*To the doors.*] Come on, hurry up in there! . . . does it on purpose . . . let you know how important he is . . . I put you there Harry! Who was it that got you the numbers? Eh Harry? Your old buddy Georgie Porter. And what did Georgie get in return? You rewarded Georgie with the ministry of Tourism! You think I care about Ayers Rock Harry? The Great Barrier Reef? You made yourself prime minister — and then you left me for dead. That's what you get for backing an old buddy in the party room — [*He returns to* ERWIN *for moral support, but* ERWIN *has become more and more absorbed in his reading, so that as* GEORGE *pauses for breath he reads the following to himself, out loud, oblivious of his boss.*]

ERWIN : [*With slight accent.*] "a living thing desires above all to vent its strength — life as such is will to power —"

GEORGE : Erwin? Erwin! Why does he want to see me *now* Erwin, why? Does he know Erwin, does he know? [*Shaking Erwin.*] That his old buddy George Porter, his faithful friend, his ally, his comrade, is slowly but surely getting the numbers — for himself! [*To the doors again.*] It's George's turn Harry! There's going to be a seesaw one day soon Harry boy — [*Lifting* ERWIN *by the collar then dropping him back again.*] — me up — and you down . . . I know what you're doing in there. You're laying Elaine, aren't you Harry? She'll be mine one day soon Harry boy . . . [*Throws tourist brochures pulled from pocket into the air.*] and *you* can look after Ayers Rock and the Barrier Reef . . . [*Turning to* ERWIN *again, who's back in his book.*] D'you think he knows? Has he smelt it out? [*Registering that* ERWIN *is not registering.*] Read read read — it's not normal. *Beyond Good and Evil.* I don't like the sound of that Erwin. By Frederick who?

ERWIN : Nietzsche. Frederick Nietzsche.

GEORGE : [*Hurling book down.*] Erwin. I bring you out, at considerable expense to the public purse, from your beer-halled, snow-capped, black-forested, cream-caked and cuckoo-clocked homeland to assist me with my portfolio, and all you read are philosophy books. We don't want that kind of thing here Erwin. Tourists! That's what we want! Tourists! Flocking and milling to this sunny, sandy, surfy, snowy, sweaty country of ours!

ERWIN : [*Producing folder.*] Cost and seat ratios per passenger kilometre, fare discount parameters, motel occupancy projections, promotional supplements in overseas newspapers — a complete plan, a package! All in six months! Everything you need Mr Porter!

GEORGE : [*Hurling folder down.*] I don't want facts, I want policies, schemes, visions! One day, Australia will replace America as the tourist mecca of the new world! One day, we'll grind America into the ground! . . . and don't keep calling me Mr Porter. We don't bow and scrape here Erwin. This is a democracy. Wolfgang is as good as his master here Erwin.

ERWIN : [*Smirks to himself, furtively.*]

GEORGE : [*Cuffing him over the ears.*] Don't smirk Erwin — try not to be so furtive and teutonic all the time. Gottlieb *is* as good as his master and [*Holding him by lapels.*] you'd better believe it. It's time you understood how Australia works.

ERWIN : This country? Work? This country — [*Says something disparaging in German.*]

GEORGE: Don't speak in German Erwin. It's okay between consenting adults in private — but not in public. Very soon Erwin, if all goes well, seat ratios and fare discounts and Ayers Rock can go to hell. [*Brandishing fist at doors.*] I'm tired of waiting Harry — you hear me? Beware the Ides of March — oops.

[*Hurries off, holding his backside, in sudden discomfort.*]

ERWIN: [*Suddenly intense, masterful, reading.*] "On the other hand: if your ship *has* been driven into these seas, very well! Clench your teeth! Keep a firm hand on the helm! We sail straight over morality and past it, we flatten, we crush what is left of our own morality by venturing to voyage thither — but what do *we* matter—"

[*Sound of toilet flushing off.*]

GEORGE : [*Returning, fixing belt.*] Ever since my wife's put us on this damned diet I have to go to the toilet about every eight minutes — or I'll explode. Muesli, pitta bread, skim milk, bran oatmeal — I've got a wheatsack moving through me in there . . . [*Resumes pacing.*] inflation is 15 per cent, unemployment seven hundred and fifty thousand, one strike after another — Harry just can't cope any more. Leadership, that's what this country needs — but not me — I know too much, don't I Harry — that's why I'm kept out in the cold. So why now Erwin? Why's he want to see me now?

[*Imperial music. Door panels open slowly.* GEORGE *steels himself for the coming encounter, while* ERWIN *goes to his knees. An impressive desk is revealed, high with papers. No one is visible behind it. Music stops.* GEORGE *moves gingerly forward.* ERWIN *does likewise, on his knees.*]

GEORGE : [*Cuffing him.*] Get up for Christ's sake. This is a democracy . . . he's not here . . . blow me down, he's asleep . . . the leader of the nation, head down on the desk . . . [*Rhetorically.*] Hop into your boats boys! Now's the time to invade! The whole bloody country, ripe for the plucking . . . [*Closer, noticing document.*] What's this? "Eyes Prime Minister only" . . . let's see if we can edge it out . . . [*Pulls gently.* HARRY'S *head falls with thump to desk top.*]

HARRY : [*Not fully aware of his surroundings, and racing around in general confusion.*] The bells! A division of the house! Tintinnabulation of the bells!

GEORGE : Sit down and calm yourself Harry — you're hearing things. [*To* ERWIN, *who has gone to his knees the moment* HARRY *has awakened.*] Don't abase yourself Erwin, for God's sake.

HARRY : It's my nerves. They're bad, really bad. The highest office in the land George! The supreme challenge! But onerous, old friend, onerous. Wears away at you like — borers in a gatepost. You like that image Mr Gruber? [ERWIN *fawns.*] The pithy phrase. The salty expression. It's a gift Mr Gruber. The ability to make a complex issue simple for the man in the street or freeway. The capacity to judge men. To size a fellow up in a second. To look right into a chap as if he were — translucent, [*He does this to* ERWIN, *who quails under his scrutiny.*] and winkle out their innermost thoughts. I suspect, Herr Gruber, that you are musical, like most of your people. [ERWIN *nods, waves his arms as if conducting, fawns.*] See George — I was right. I shall hum a tune — see if you can identify it. [*He hums a tune, continues, gets lost in it — it's a slow, dreamy tune — and goes off into a daydream, as if unaware of their presence.* ERWIN *tries to tiptoe away.*]

GEORGE : Come back, you dolt, he's just gone into one of his brown studies... he'll snap out of it in a moment... [*Confidentially.*] personally, I think he's on the verge of nervous collapse.

HARRY: [*Slowly coming round, but not fully with them. He declaims, as if in the middle of a speech.*] If elected, my government... eh? Ah, still there George. What can I do for you?

GEORGE : *You* wanted to see *me*, Harry.

HARRY : I did?... Elaine! Elaine!

[*Enter* ELAINE. *They whisper. As they confer, he touches, strokes her arm, making discreet advances. She, just as discreetly, fends him off. He gets slightly more importunate, forcing her to exit. He watches her going, then goes off into another reverie, obviously about her. After a brief consultation,* GEORGE *and* ERWIN *decide to tiptoe off. They're almost off when* HARRY *comes to again and rushes about as before.*]

HARRY : The bells! It's a division! The tintinnabulation of 'em!

GEORGE : I don't hear any bells Harry. [*To* ERWIN.] He's got them in his head.

HARRY : [*Recovering and remembering reason for interview.*] Mujik [*He pronounces it moojik.*] George. What's it mean to you?

GEORGE : [*Uneasy, looking at* ERWIN *for assistance.*] A type of sled used in the Carpathians? [HARRY *shakes his head.*] A contagious skin condition common amongst reindeer? [HARRY *shakes his head.*] A whalebone banjo used by Eskimos?

HARRY : [*Impatiently.*] Come on George. It's just been invaded by Russia.

GEORGE : Aha — you mean Mujik. [*He pronounces it Mudjik.*] Mujik's been invaded by Russia.

HARRY : Mujik. [*Moojik.*]

GEORGE : Mujik. [*Mudjik.*]

HARRY : George, I haven't got all day. Mujik, as you know, is a satrap of the Soviet Union—

GEORGE : A what Harry?

HARRY : A satrap George. Mujik's a satrap.

GEORGE : [*Consulting with* ERWIN.] A Himalayan snow leopard? A Sherpa sandal made from blubber fat?

HARRY : George, inflation and unemployment are rising. I don't have time to waste. What is it exactly you want to see me about?

GEORGE : I'm sorry Harry, but you asked to see me.

HARRY : About what George?

GEORGE : About Mujik Harry. [*Pronounced Mudjik.*]

HARRY : What's that? A triple-stringed ukelele used in the Urals? A by-product of polar bear's liver?

GEORGE : [*Giving up.*] About Mujik Harry. [*Pronounced Moojik.*]

HARRY : George, as you know, Mujik has just become Russia's vassal.

GEORGE : There's no water in those parts Harry. No water at all.

HARRY : Vassal, George, vassal. We have a bit of a problem on our hands, and you could be the man to solve it. A Mr Percha, Mujik's trade minister, is on his way to Australia. He is going to try to dissuade us from putting an embargo on our wool exports to his country. We know, and he knows, that

American pressure on us to do this is increasing all the time. Eventually we're going to have to bow to that pressure. But not yet. Our strategy is to hold out against America as long as possible. So what you do with Mr Percha is stall. Don't give him a definite answer. It's very delicate George, and I'll tell you why. We can't promise Mujik anything, but we can't offend them either. Mujik's a pretty small place, but strategic — it's a buffer state. And you know what that means ... you do know what that means George?

[GEORGE *looks blank.*]

HARRY : [*Getting up and positioning* GEORGE *and* ERWIN *back to back,* ERWIN *quietly quivering with terror at his approach.*] I know you're not Foreign Affairs George, but I would have thought you'd have known about a buffer state. [*He crouches, runs and butts* ERWIN, *terrified, in the stomach.*] ... I am Russia George, you are China, and Herr Gruber here in the middle is Mujik — in other words — [*Butting him again.*] a buffer ... [HARRY, *dazed by the impact on his head, holds his temples, wanders a moment, sits, and goes into another reverie.*]

ERWIN : Mr Shanahan is sick ... I will get blame!

GEORGE : Mr Shanahan is mad Erwin — and very soon I hope to be in his place. Mr Shanahan is not fit to govern.

HARRY : [*Droning, as if in parliament.*] Clause seven of this Bill seeks not to exterminate the much-loved kangaroo, but only to cull it — before our pastures are eaten out from under us by this ungainly but ever-popular marsupial ... [*Comes to.*]

GEORGE : Yes Harry, but why me? Why not the minister for trade to greet Mr Percha?

HARRY : Because I want this low-profile George. And because Mr Percha has Tourism in his portfolio as well as Trade. We have agreed that the pretext for his visit will be to tell us of the attractions of his cold, ugly, sloping, windswept, breath-condensing land. But really, he wants us to keep sending them our wool. So handle him carefully. Your welcome must be courteous and yet cool, affable yet impassive, imperceptible yet discernible, cordial yet— [*Running out of alternatives.*]

ERWIN : Aloof.

HARRY : Genial and yet—
ERWIN : Restrained.
HARRY : Amicable yet—
ERWIN : Subdued.
  [*Imperial music begins quietly. Doors start slowly closing.*
  GEORGE *and* ERWIN *get up and start retreating, facing him
  respectfully the whole time.*]
HARRY : [*Already immersed in other matters.*] How's Barbara?
GEORGE : [*Walking backward, music gradually up, lights gra-
  dually down.*] Fine, fine.
HARRY : And the boys?
GEORGE : Ball of muscle.
  [*Music up. Doors close. Lights down.*]

SCENE 2

*Two chairs and a table, set with a frugal-looking meal of pieces
of middle-eastern bread stuffed with salad vegetables. The meal
organized,* BARBARA PORTER *is practising Tai Chi movements from
an instruction book.*

BARBARA : [*Reading aloud.*] "Counter-clockwise turn. [*She
  pivots 180°.*] Pivot 90° on the right heel. The right foot
  now points to the south. Pivot on the left heel, with the toe
  pointing up [*She's getting into difficulties.*] so that the left
  toe now points east. [*She finds balance difficult.*] Now
  turn your body to the left and move the arms in front of the
  body with the right vertical fist placed over the left elbow.
  The left open palm [*More difficulties.*] is facing you, and
  under the right elbow. The hands are held as though carrying a rectangular box." [*She is now in a rather awkward
  ritualized posture.*]
  [*Enter* GEORGE, *who inspects her without speaking.*]
BARBARA : [*Abstractedly, determinedly.*] Carry Tiger to Mountain.
GEORGE : [*Miming her movements.*] Carry husband's dinner to
  table.
BARBARA : [*Moving arms in rhythmic, weaving motion.*] The
  Simple Develops Naturally into the Manifold.

GEORGE : [*Miming her again.*] Slight pangs develop naturally into ravenous appetite.

BARBARA : [*Grimly persisting*] The Primal Powers Never Come to a Standstill!

GEORGE : The rumblings of the stomach are as thunder in the valleys!

BARBARA : Damn you! I've lost it!

GEORGE : You and your Tai Chi — I'm sick of it. All this:— [*Gyrating and wheeling about.*] "Wave Your Hands like Clouds/Open Gates to Kingdom Within/Carry Tiger to Mountain/Move over the Waves like a Sea Serpent nonsense!

BARBARA : Fifteen years ago we had a nice house in Melbourne, a weekender in the country, friends, parties, restaurants — then you decided you had to go into politics. I *have* to do Tai Chi to stay sane.

GEORGE : [*Holding up salad-filled bread.*] Someone's filled the diplomatic bag with raw vegetables.

BARBARA : [*Ignoring this and proceeding.*] You had to compete with your old buddy Harry Shanahan. Everything he did, you had to do better. Fifteen years of hatching and huddling in smoke-filled rooms — and he's prime minister and you've got Tourism.

GEORGE : Are you posting this salad? Why is it in a jiffy bag? I want my dinner.

BARBARA : Fifteen years of slapping or stabbing backs and what have you got? Ayers Rock! That *is* your dinner.

GEORGE : I want roast lamb and gravy and baked potatoes! Why do you always have to copy the latest fad from America?

BARBARA : There's only one way these long, lost Canberra years are going to be worth it. That's when you get where you said you would. To the top! And that will be never. Harry Shanahan's beaten you to it.

GEORGE : I'm always hungry! I'm filled with wheatgerm and soyabean and lentils. My intestine is a conveyor belt.

BARBARA : Look out that window George. See those tents out there on Capitol Hill? The unemployed are camped there George — hundreds of them. Harry can't cope! Now's your chance! Make your move! See him!

GEORGE : [*Attacking food unwillingly.*] *He* saw *me* today.

BARBARA : So he knows you're getting the numbers.

GEORGE : If he does he's playing it cool. He wants me to welcome someone — one of Mujik's top ministers. They're worried we're going to embargo our wool exports and they'll all freeze to death . . . this tastes like a post office.

BARBARA : If he's one of Mujik's top ministers, why's he want *you* to do it?

GEORGE : Thank you. Because he's also minister for Tourism and he's pretending to be out here for travel talks.

BARBARA : What? You tub of lard — you temple gong — it's a set up. Harry wants you to be seen with a senior Communist minister, a Russian stooge. You and him, shaking hands, all over the front pages — George Porter and Communism, linked in the public mind.

GEORGE : It will be low profile. I'll be courteous yet subdued, affable yet cool, genial yet aloof, imperceptible yet discernible, cordial and yet [*Still chewing away, disgruntled.*] inedible.

BARBARA : The news is sure to get out. And Mujik is bad news.

GEORGE : I've got it all worked out. I'm meeting him at the Air Force Base. Press not allowed. I have an urgent call!

BARBARA : All you need is one photographer — George Porter and the Russian puppet in loving embrace. The press'll make muesli of you.

GEORGE : [*Hurrying off in discomfort.*] Don't say muesli! Don't even mention the word!

BARBARA : Don't you ever stay put! You're too tense!

GEORGE : [*Going.*] It's your damned gravel and cardboard — it's on the move again! I'll have to welcome this guy on a commode!

[*Slow fade as* BARBARA, *shaking her head, starts on her meal.*]

SCENE 3

Airport steps at side of stage.
Enter, slightly formally, ERWIN, *carrying a large ceremonial alphenhorn,* BARBARA, *carrying a toy koala, and* GEORGE, *in a strange tribal hat.*

GEORGE : I've studied their damned economy, their history, their culture, their geography, some of their idiot phrases, but the hat — I object to the hat — I look ridiculous.

BARBARA : But not to Mr Percha.

ERWIN : Worn by village headman to welcome herdsmen down from the hills. Great compliment.

GEORGE : We're going to too much trouble. We're supposed to be courteous yet subdued, affable yet cool, genial yet aloof—

BARBARA : The strategy makes sense. This man is a Russian stooge. So when we welcome him in traditional tribal trappings —

ERWIN : We remind him of the civilization he's helping to destroy. So ingenious, if you permit me [*Blows on alphenhorn.*] to blow own trumpet. Seems like welcome. Actually rebuff!

BARBARA : Quote your Mujik proverb to me George.

GEORGE : [*Gabbling gibberish*] . . . No man qualifies as a statesman who is ignorant of the avalanche.

BARBARA : Handle this right and you can quote it to Harry Shanahan as well. We'll welcome him, yet separate ourselves from him — Harry'll get snowed! Right, let's have a dry run. I'll be Percha coming down the steps — and remember not to talk about the weather with him.

GEORGE : Why not the weather? What the hell else can I talk about?

ERWIN : Theirs is so terrible that to talk of it is to remind them of it. Considered a grave insult in their country.

BARBARA : [*From top of stairs.*] Come on, come on.

GEORGE : Once through this damned fool routine is enough.

ERWIN : Their quaint national anthem!

[*Music.* BARBARA *and* ERWIN *move from one foot to the other.* GEORGE *stands rigidly to attention.*]

BARBARA : Can't you remember anything? If you stand still in Mujik for more than thirty seconds you freeze to death.

[*The three of them move from one foot to the other as music proceeds briefly. Then* BARBARA *comes down steps.*]

ERWIN : The horn Mr Porter! The horn!

[*Porter puts it to his lips reluctantly.*]

GEORGE : Yuk. Tastes like prehistoric asparagus. [*Blows.*]

BARBARA : An authentic, traditional, non-communist welcome. It'll blow the little sherpa's mind.

ERWIN: [*Directing.*] He will pause at the bottom of the steps and you move towards him.
[GEORGE *does so.*]
BARBARA: No, you fool, sideways! Sidle man, sidle!
ERWIN: [*While* GEORGE *sidles.*] Derives, according to National Geographic Magazine, from their desire to present as little of themselves as possible to the icy winds of the region — bear hug now — as if to keep him warm — then you make your little welcoming speech, Mrs Porter makes marsupial presentation, and off you go.
[*Landing . . . roar of plane.*]
BARBARA: He's coming!
[*Enter TV man with shoulder camera, trying to look unobtrusive.*]
GEORGE: [*Using alphenhorn.*] No you don't. Out you go my inquisitive friend! How'd you get in?
TV MAN: [*Trying to shoot* GEORGE.] Please! I beg you! It's too good to miss!
GEORGE: They'll think I'm one of the Muppets.
TV MAN: A few seconds, please!
GEORGE: Out! Out!
TV MAN: Three million viewers! The lead story!
GEORGE: All laughing their heads off! [*He's driven off.*]
[*More anthem sounds.* PERCHA, *in fur hat, dark suit and large cufflinks, appears at top of steps, and moves from one foot to the other with the anthem as do the welcomers. Then he waves, comes down steps.* GEORGE *lifts alphenhorn to lips,* PERCHA *flinches, as if expecting it to go off, then listens to the strange noises.* GEORGE *finishes, says "Here we go" to* ERWIN, *and sidles in short steps to* PERCHA, *who tries to conceal his bewilderment. As* GEORGE *attempts bear hug,* PERCHA, *thinking he is being attacked, karates him with a loud hah!* GEORGE *falls.*]
ERWIN: [*Rushing forward waving* National Geographic.]
Official Mujik greeting! *National Geographic!*
PERCHA: Not used since 1939! [*Picks up* GEORGE.] A thousand apologies. Terrible mistake! Diplomatic disaster! *This* correct Mujik greeting . . . [*Whacking* GEORGE *across face.*] "May your frozen cheekbones once again tingle" — old saying. So! Sorry, sorry.

GEORGE : Well, anyway, welcome to our country. And welcome from our country to your country. And welcome to your country for offering welcome to our country. Our country welcomes overtures of welcome from your country. Your country — [*He pauses, tied in his own verbal knot.* ERWIN *whispers, nudges.*] — as they say in your country — [*He gabbles his Mujik saying.* PERCHA *breaks up.*]

ERWIN : [*Nervously to* PERCHA.] No man qualifies as a statesman who is ignorant of the avalanche?

PERCHA : No, no what he say means — forgive — a thousand apologies — bawdy — ribaldness — rudery — it means I am climbing the mountain, see, up here — [*Demonstrates on steps.*] — you are climbing also — down here. I, up here, about to — about to — deference to womenfolk — [*Whispers to* ERWIN, *who whispers to* GEORGE.] — so I yell [*He bellows out some gibberish.*] — in order to warn you below, understand?

BARBARA : [*Trying to retrieve situation.*] Allow me to present you with this enchanting toy koala . . .

GEORGE : When its quaint little eye is pressed, Waltzing Matilda sounds forth.

ERWIN : From Australian-made transistor embedded in the furry creature's tiny pouch.

[PERCHA *presses.* Waltzing Matilda. *All stand to attention. Lights down.*]

SCENE 4

GEORGE, BARBARA, ERWIN *and* PERCHA *sit waiting outside the prime ministerial doors.* ERWIN *is absorbed in his Nietzsche book, and sits somewhat apart from the rest. He reads parts to himself, occasionally out loud —*

ERWIN : "Independence — a privilege of the strong! And he who attempts it — *proves* that he is strong! . . ."

[*They stare at him. He stops, embarrassed.*]

GEORGE : I'm not sure about all this — Mr Shanahan's a very busy man.

PERCHA : Please, I beg. Essential. [*Touching socks, pants, etc.*] This from your wool. This. This. Without it, freeze — I make plea — busy man — of course — I make plea about wool. [*Squashing up next to* BARBARA.] Your lady look beautiful in wool.

[*Sounds of giggles, screams within.*]

BARBARA : [*To* GEORGE, *but quite audible.*] Disgusting old pi s hng Elaine.

PERCHA : Elaine? Chased?

ERWIN : [*Looking up from book.*] Impossible for prime minister's secretary to be chaste.

GEORGE : [*Going over to him and cuffing him.*] Very funny.

BARBARA : Isn't it disgusting? Unemployment and inflation galloping away and he's chasing Elaine.

ERWIN : Elaine was chaste. Long time ago.

GEORGE : [*Whacking him again.*] Stop trying to be funny. Germans have no sense of humour! [GEORGE *suddenly grabs his backside, grimaces, and hurries off.*]

PERCHA : What matter with him?

ERWIN : Expects fresh bombing attack of special diet. Therefore evacuate bowel.

BARBARA : [*Going over and cuffing him.*] I'll tell George that.

[*Noises get worse.*]

BARBARA : This is outrageous! She's being raped.

[*She goes up to doors, opens them, to sound of imperial music.* HARRY *has* ELAINE *down on the desk. He desists.* ELAINE *smacks his face. So does* BARBARA, *and so does* PERCHA, *thinking he's doing the right thing.*]

PERCHA : May your frozen cheekbones once again tingle.

HARRY : [*Whacking him back.*] And the same to you.

ELAINE : [*Being consoled and helped off by* BARBARA.] I'm not taking any more of his shorthand or his uncontrollable longhand.

HARRY : Elaine! Don't leave me!

[*Flushing sounds off. Enter* GEORGE, *adjusting his pants.*]

GEORGE : Mr Shanahan. This is Mr Percha from Mujik . . . I'm sorry Harry, but he insisted. I said maybe five minutes. Five minutes and no more.

[HARRY *turns half away in irritation.*]

PERCHA : [*Trying to mollify him.*] Have gift for you. And you. And you.

GEORGE : [*As they all unwrap their little gifts.*] What are these, exactly?

PERCHA : This is coggle.

HARRY : Coggle eh? All the way from Mujik.

[GEORGE *consults quietly with* ERWIN *as they unwrap.* ER-WIN *shakes his head. It is obvious none of them know what they are.*]

PERCHA : Great delicacy. Favourite sweetmeat on snowy slopes. Supreme confection.

[PERCHA *pops it into his mouth with relish. The others do likewise. They seem to be enjoying them in a guarded sort of way. As they're chewing and expressing polite approbation,* PERCHA *explains.*]

PERCHA : From the yak, our national creature, nothing is wasted. Fur, skin, meat, horns, bones. Even eyes. Eyes of dead yak removed, dried, smoked, hung up for one year, two, three, then dipped in sugar — [*Pauses.*]

HARRY : [*Interested.*] Dipped in sugar eh?

PERCHA : Then in chocolate — become — coggles.

[*They go through various routines of getting rid of them furtively, yet fast. By this time* PERCHA *has seated himself opposite the prime minister at his desk and shoots his cuffs in a strange way whenever he thinks he's unobserved. He takes advantage of their discomfort to begin a speech.*]

PERCHA : The government of Mujik pay compliments to the government of Australia. For long time people of Mujik have great curiosity about people of Australia. Seem unfair to people of Mujik that wool flourish in hot flat place when needed by cold sloping place. But that is how cookie — how cookie — decomposes.

GEORGE : Crumbles. How cookie crumbles.

[*By now* HARRY's *gone off into a daydream.*]

PERCHA : What happened?

GEORGE : Brown study.

PERCHA : [*Looking around at walls.*] True, but what's matter with occupant of brown study?

GEORGE : Nervous strain. Australia land of sun, sand, surf, snow and many problems.

PERCHA : Wool - must tell him — without wool we goosepimple.

GEORGE : [*Beckoning for the two of them to follow him out.*] You know about meditation in your country? Well, he's meditating.

PERCHA: [*Backing out reluctantly.*] Must tell him about wool! Must tell him!
[HARRY, *now in a doze, lets his head drop so that it bumps desk.*]
HARRY: [*Getting up and rushing about.*] Bells! Division bells! Tintinnabulation of 'em!
GEORGE: Calm down Harry. There're no bells.
HARRY: Phew. Must be the heat. What's the weather like over there? [PERCHA *stiffens, clicks heels, bows, storms out.*] What's the matter with him?
GEORGE: Didn't anyone brief you Harry? It's an insult to ask 'em about their weather, because it's so awful ... Did you notice something funny about his cuffs? They way he shot them all the time?
HARRY: No I did not. And don't bring him in again. He's your responsibility, George. News of this little meeting could get out. I don't want to be associated with this business in any way.
GEORGE: Something funny about his cufflinks ...
[HARRY *becomes preoccupied with his work. Music starts, doors start closing. They retreat from his presence backwards.*]
HARRY: How's Barbara?
GEORGE: Fine, fine.
HARRY: And the boys?
GEORGE: Ball of muscle.
[*They exit, just in time. Lights down as* GEORGE *shoots his cuffs the way he's seen* PERCHA *do it, meditatively, as if he's on the verge of something.*]

SCENE 5

BARBARA *is doing tai chi movements, reading from her instruction book again.*

BARBARA: "From the Single Whip Posture, pivot the left foot, now pointing east, 90° to point south. Bend the right knee and bring the whole body down, squatting to the right —"
[*She's having difficulties.*] — "Keep your feet parallel and

heels flat on the ground . . . move the extended left hand —"
[*She gets cramp in leg.*] — George! George! O God!
[*Enter* GEORGE.]
GEORGE : [*Helping her release herself from cramped posture and massaging her leg.*] Bloody Tai Chi! It's supposed to relax you, and all you get are cramps . . . listen, I'm really onto something. Something really big . . . the coup of the decade.
BARBARA : Please! [*Indicating painful area.*] Concentrate!
GEORGE : [*Not concentrating.*] If I'm right, this is finally going to get me the numbers in the party room . . . we'll be able to get rid of Harry and I'll take his place — swept in on a wave of popular feeling!
BARBARA : O I'll do it. [*She does her own massage, which isn't easy as the spot on her foot is inaccessible.*]
GEORGE : Percha — is a spy! He's not out here for trade or tourism. What did you notice about his cufflinks? [*Helping her rub the sole of her foot.*] His cufflinks were unusually large. And when he sat down at Harry's desk, he did this [*Demonstrating.*] all the time over his papers. They're cameras!
BARBARA : You're crazy.
GEORGE : His cufflinks are tiny cameras. He wasn't shooting his cuffs — he was shooting pictures. And Erwin is bringing him here right now after a monstrous four-hour lunch. These Mujik fellows are prodigious drinkers. He'll be blotto — absolutely rotten. We'll top him up, then you can have a dance with him or something and work it off his sleeve.
BARBARA : You dance with him — you can make a fool of yourself, not me.
GEORGE : You've got to do it. He likes you. He wants to take you back and feed you on coggles and cabbage for the rest of your life.
BARBARA : No!
GEORGE : Yes!
[*Enter* ERWIN *and* PERCHA, *both drunk.* PERCHA *is singing a strange Mujik song,* ERWIN *crooning a German one.* ERWIN *goes over to* BARBARA *and tries to dance with her.* PERCHA *goes over to* GEORGE *and does likewise.*]
PERCHA : In Mujik, the men dance with the men!
[*They caper together,* GEORGE *trying to work the cufflinks*

off his sleeve, without success. PERCHA, *drunk and giddy, falls over.*]

PERCHA : Not used to flatness! Used to sloping! The mountain goat sprains his fetlock on the plains!

[*He gets up and cuts in on* ERWIN, *who's dancing with unwilling* BARBARA. *This sends* ERWIN *into the arms of* GEORGE. *They dance for a few second, then* ERWIN, *unable to cope with the familiarity, gets an attack of the cringes.*]

GEORGE : Get a whiskey into him.

[ERWIN *pours and offers* PERCHA *a large whiskey, which he takes while dancing, downs in a Slavonic gulp.* BARBARA *whirls him around.* PERCHA *falls to the floor and passes out.*]

GEORGE : A cufflink! Quickly!

[GEORGE *gets it off him and races off in triumph. Seizing his chance,* ERWIN *again approaches* BARBARA *with a German lovesong.*]

BARBARA : Please Erwin. You've had too much to drink.

ERWIN : Please! I beg!

[*They dance,* BARBARA *unwilling. In the process,* PERCHA's *hand is trodden on. He stirs, and in an obviously instinctive gesture checks his sleeve, gropes, wakes, realizes it is missing, gets up as if electrified, rushes about, looking frantically.*]

PERCHA : I have lost! O, I have lost!

[*As he rushes off one side,* GEORGE *rushes in the other.*]

GEORGE : It's a camera! I was right!

BARBARA : Look out — he's coming back!

[*As* GEORGE *rushes off,* PERCHA *rushes on.*]

PERCHA : I have lost! O, I have lost!

BARBARA & ERWIN : [*Together.*] What have you lost? What? What?

PERCHA : Personal! Private! At restaurant perhaps!

[PERCHA *rushes off.* GEORGE *rushes on.*]

GEORGE : I was right! I'll be on the front page of every paper in the land! [*Giving cufflink to* BARBARA.] Take a photo of your next prime minister!

[*Blackout.*]

SCENE 6

GEORGE *appears at side of stage, running on the spot, limbering up, and peeling off his jacket and trousers.*

GEORGE : [*To* BARBARA, *in wings.*] My shirt — where's my old tee shirt?

BARBARA : [*Unseen.*] Don't do it! Don't be so stupid.

GEORGE : [*Changing.*] If he wants a game, I'll give him a game. My shirt!

BARBARA : [*Throwing it at him.*] You haven't played for months and months.

GEORGE : Neither has he.

BARBARA : [*Emerging, with white socks, runners.*] So why now — why's he asked you?

GEORGE : It's his way of talking things over — he knows I'm getting the numbers. He'll try to square off — offer me favours.

BARBARA : He's lethal on the squash court.

GEORGE : I know. [*Touching ear.*] I've still got the scar from last time.

BARBARA : He's lethal — and he's furious with you.

GEORGE : Pushed him off the front page for five days. The great spy scandal.

BARBARA : You're a threat to him. Be careful.

GEORGE : He'll try to buy me off. High Commissioner to London. That type of thing. How'd you like to live in London?

BARBARA : Not now, no.

GEORGE : Thought you hated Canberra.

BARBARA : I'd love Canberra if I ruled over it.

GEORGE : [*Equipped and ready, with racket.*] I'm within — striking distance.

[HARRY, *similarly equipped, jogs out from the other side.*]

HARRY : Aha — all ready for a thrashing?

GEORGE : You always say that — and I always win.

HARRY : Aggression and confidence George. The secret of leadership. [*Taps head*] That's where the battle's won. I thought I won last time?

GEORGE : I won . . . but you beat me — across the head.

[*They start playing.*]

HARRY : Sorry — got a bit carried away.

GEORGE : Same here — knocked unconscious.

HARRY: Not with you.

GEORGE: You got carried away — so I got carried away.

HARRY: Aha yes. Pun. That's two puns to you and two points to me.

[*Tempo increases. They get more monosyllabic.*]

GEORGE : You're winning.

HARRY : Like to win.

GEORGE : Noticed that.

HARRY : That Percha business. Way you went about it. Damned clever. Deal well with foreigners.

GEORGE : Ah!

HARRY : Job for you. Top post. Prestige. Travel.

GEORGE : High Commissioner, London.

HARRY : How'd you know?

GEORGE : Second sight.

HARRY: Striped pants. Rolls Royce. Right people. Receptions. Queen. Balls.

GEORGE: Exactly.

HARRY : Eh?

GEORGE : Balls.

HARRY: I'm sorry?

GEORGE: Prefer Canberra.

HARRY : What's the score?

GEORGE : About even.

HARRY: Unemployment. You. Minister for Industrial Relations. Big challenge. Portfolio of the future. Tip out Black Jack. Move you in.

GEORGE : And you. On top still.

HARRY : Like to, yes.

GEORGE: Remember our schooldays? Your gang and my gang. Your gang not quite as big as my gang. You propose merger. Soon, you leader of both gangs.

HARRY : Play things hard. My nature.

GEORGE : My gang getting bigger than your gang. Again.

HARRY : Your gang?

GEORGE : Party room gang.

HARRY : What's the score?

GEORGE : I could be winning.

HARRY: Doubt it. Storm brewing. Percha photographed secret document. From America. Complete embargo plans for Mujik. America'll blame us for leak — carelessness.

GEORGE: But I uncovered it!

HARRY: If you hadn't, they'd never have known where leak came from.

GEORGE: So it's my fault.

HARRY: In a way, yes.

GEORGE: Our colleagues don't think so.

HARRY: Who's winning?

GEORGE: Me.

HARRY: Since when?

GEORGE: Since this morning. Head count. Thirty-eight to me, thirty-six to you. So America can go to blazes. New foreign policy. Tired of kissing their arses.

HARRY: You wouldn't! — Me?

GEORGE: I would — you. Thirty-eight to thirty-six.

HARRY: You wouldn't.

GEORGE: Would!

HARRY: Then I would too. [*Moving towards him with racquet up.*] With this wood I would. My turn to pun, George. With this wood I [*Lunges, swishes.*] would.

GEORGE: [*Defending.*] Not with you Harry.

HARRY: Not for much longer, George, no.

[*They duel.* GEORGE *first defends, then takes offensive. He gets carried away and finally strikes* HARRY *down. During which —*]

GEORGE: Country's falling apart. Unemployment. Strikes. Inflation. Americans telling us what to do and when to do it. I'm the man of the hour Harry. They want me in the party room. Call me Mr Mujik. You can have tourism.

HARRY: [*Fighting back.*] Tired of you sniping. Yapping at my heels. I'm sorry George.

GEORGE: So am I Harry.

[HARRY *is struck down. Blackout.*]

SCENE 7

GEORGE, *in squash clothes plus black jacket, is practising an address to the nation sitting down in front of a mirror, as if on TV.*

GEORGE: Ladies and gentlemen — that doesn't sound right — men and women of Australia — sounds like the Labor Party — hello there — too informal. Fellow Australians — that's better — why, you are no doubt wondering, am I addressing you in mourning costume late this afternoon. I have taken the liberty of interrupting "Gilligan's Island" and other family favourites to bring you news of an extremely serious nature. Let us take this in stimple seps — simple steps —

BARBARA : [*Entering.*] Come on — you're facing the nation in five minutes!

GEORGE : I can't get it right!

BARBARA : It's your finest hour!

GEORGE : My insides are a jelly! [*Racing off.*] Here comes the oatmeal avalanche!

BARBARA : [*After him.*] Listen. You're upset — that's natural. Everyone's upset. But get it right — show you've got what it takes — and you're prime minister. The sympathy for your predicament is tremendous. To be — accidentally responsible for the death of the man you could well have succeeded anyway — *quelle delicatesse!* — what emotions you can inspire!

GEORGE : [*Returning, adjusting pants, to sounds of flushing.*] "I'm sorry George".

BARBARA : Stop it George.

GEORGE : They were his last words. We grew up together. Played football together — law school together.

BARBARA : You hated him! Every TV and radio station in Australia is about to stand by — for you. You can build yourself an image that'll keep you going for years . . .
[*Light up on other side of stage. A chair, table, TV camera.* DIRECTOR *fusses with camera.* ERWIN *fusses with props. As he does so, he mumbles bits of Nietzsche to himself, occasionally out loud, but takes hold of himself when the director stares at him strangely.*]

ERWIN : "Where the people eat and drink, even where they worship, there is usually a stink . . . one should not go into churches if one wants to breathe pure air . . ."

BARBARA : To unwittingly cause the death of an old friend whom fate decrees you must succeed! Tragedy! Greek tragedy!

GEORGE : Lies! I'll tell them the truth!

BARBARA : He attacked you. You did it in self defence.

GEORGE : After the defence came offence. I lost control of myself. I killed him.

BARBARA : You hit him on the head accidentally while you were playing. Say it!

GEORGE : [*Pointing to cut over eyebrow.*] And what about this?

BARBARA : [*Producing them and putting them on him.*] Sunglasses! [*She pulls him across into the TV lights.* ERWIN *fawns. The Director stares at him aghast.*]

BARBARA : [*To* GEORGE.] Get it right — and the job is yours!

DIRECTOR : He looks terrible!

BARBARA : That's how he's got to be — ravaged! He was his best friend.

DIRECTOR : He looks like a debilitated parrot! Sixty seconds!

GEORGE : [*Getting up and removing glasses.*] I can't do it! I can't see properly!

BARBARA : [*Pushing him back and replacing glasses.*] They've got to see *you!*

DIRECTOR : Your cards ready? Racquet? Koala? Forty-five seconds.

BARBARA : Be simple — straightforward — unrehearsed — overcome with emotion.

GEORGE : [*Getting up again.*] I'm nervous! I want to go to the toilet!

DIRECTOR : Thirty seconds! We'll have to sedate him! . . . Twenty-five seconds! [GEORGE *tries to get up again.* BARBARA *whacks him on the head with the squash racquet. Stunned, he sits there.*]

DIRECTOR : Action!

GEORGE : Fellow Australians — late good afternoon. I'm sorry, good late afternoon. After the unfortunate events of the last few days, I think I can safely say that I need no introduction. My name, for those of you who have been out of town, is George F. Porter. I have taken the liberty of depriving you of "Gilligan's Island", the "Brady Bunch" (repeat) and other indigenous favourites to bring you some news of the utmost gravity. Let me make two simple points. [*Holding up card with 1 on it.*] One: why I, instead of your prime minister, appear before you so late this afternoon — this so late afternoon — an afternoon as late as this. And, [*Holding up 2 card.*] two: why you see me in this somewhat unusual attire. The truth is that I have some tragic news to convey to you today. Tragic for you, the ordinary people of Australia, and doubly tragic for me. Why only tragic for you and [*Holding up card with 1 x 2 on it.*] doubly tragic for me? Because I was not only Harry Shanahan's colleague but also his friend. His oldest friend. We worked together and played together. Football. Cricket. Tennis. Regrettably, another game is the cause of my appearing before you this afternoon late — this late afternoon — [*Produces squash racquet.*] — it was with a weapon — I'm sorry, a racquet of this kind, in the course of a vigorous but friendly sporting contest with Mr Shanahan, that I accidentally, in an attempt to retrieve a back wall shot, to return which, as those of you who have played the game — the game of squash — will know, requires a shot of great vigour — [*Pauses, lost, wipes sunglasses, tries again.*] — it was in attempting to retrieve a tricky long shot from my opponent that I executed a stroke — let me put that another way — I hit the right honourable gentleman very hard — accidentally hit the right honourable gentleman as hard as I could — on the very spot where a man of his eminence — or, indeed, any man for that matter, is most vulnerable — with the result that — as a result of the blow delivered forcefully but accidentally in the heat of the moment — Mr Shanahan was caused an injury which I have no option to call other than fatal — in short, he died of it. And so [*Producing koala and holding it to his chest.*] bear with me — see? While I press its charming little eye as a mark of respect for the great man. [*He stands. "Waltzing Matilda" sounds. He shows signs of discomfort.*]

DIRECTOR: Cut!

BARBARA: You've done it! It's ours!

GEORGE: Oh! [*Rushes off into wings holding backside.*]

[*Blackout.*]

SCENE 8

ERWIN *paces downstage, before the prime ministerial doors, absorbed in his philosophy book.*

ERWIN : "Every profound spirit needs a mask! Around every profound spirit a mask is continually growing, thanks to the constantly false interpretation of every word, every step, every sign of life he gives —"

GEORGE : [*Entering and catching him at it.*] How — how can you possibly — your head in a philosophy book — when it's all here! Mine! The whole bleeding lot of it! You won't have time for your beloved Nitch or Notch I promise you. Open up dem pearly gates!

[*Presses switch. Imperial music. Doors open.* ERWIN *bows instinctively at the spectacle.* GEORGE *goes up to the empty desk but stays on the wrong side of it, addressing his imaginary self in the chair.*]

Knew you had it in you Georgie boy! Old G.P., the kid from Glenhuntly Road! [*Round to chair.*] Georgie Porter's going to show 'em — the papers, the smart-arse commentators, the Labor party, the unions — leadership! That's what you're going to get! This country, Erwin, has been drifting too long! Get out there and prepare me some position papers — unemployment, inflation, Australian/American relations! Let's have some action round here! [ERWIN *scurries off.* GEORGE *continues, to himself.*] You're fired — and you're hired! I can do anything I want! Havana cigars! Johnny Walker Black Label! And [*Pressing button on desk.*] the greatest prize of all — Elaine!

ELAINE : [*Entering rather hesitantly.*] Sir?

GEORGE : Sir? Call me George — Georgie. We're going to be friends — close friends . . . sit down, sit down . . . what a moment! The first cuckoo in spring — and my maiden memo! Who'll I fire it at? Who do I hate?

ELAINE : Before you do sir —

GEORGE : George — Georgie — the name you — and only you — will call me.

ELAINE : There's all this Harry left behind — Georgie.

GEORGE : Harry? Harry?

ELAINE : He asked me to call him that Georgie.

GEORGE : O he did, did he? Well he's Mr Shanahan from now on. [*Going through papers.*] My God, there's stacks of it ... petition from the unemployed — I'm sick and tired of the unemployed! Report from the International Fatty Acid Conference ... here, let's start with this one. Request from the Japanese Collapsible Bicycle Promotion Institute ... [*Dictates.*] ... "Collapsible Sirs" — go on, write it down, write it down, let's give our foreign policy a shot in the arm — "re your request for an import licence for your patented velocipedes" — send 'em to the dictionary, why not? — "I wish to point out that I find the whole notion of the Japanese bicycle unacceptable, redolent as it is" — yes, redolent, that'll have them scratching their heads — "of memories of wartime Singapore." — You look beautiful today. [*Making advances.*]

ELAINE : Now now Mr Porter —

GEORGE : Georgie —

ELAINE : Please Georgie —

GEORGE : O we *are* getting familiar. [ELAINE *retreats round desk. He pursues. Enter* ERWIN. GEORGE *pretends it's a jogging exercise.*] Jog-jog-jog — that's all we're doing Erwin — fitness — essential — Elaine is fit — I am fit — all my staff must be fit.

ERWIN : [*Perhaps jogging behind them.*] Sir! — Mein Herr!

GEORGE : Don't revert Erwin, don't revert —

ERWIN : The American ambassador awaits without.

GEORGE : [*Stopping, puffed.*] Phew. Who do you think I am Erwin, *Henry IV Part One?*

ERWIN : Wants to see you at once!

GEORGE : At once? Who does he think he is? Tell him to wait. [*Exit* ERWIN, *looking distressed ... resuming dictation.*] To the Australian Stuffed Animal Association — "Gentlemen. Thank you for your kind remarks about my use of your electrified koala; however —" What a beautiful forearm you have. [*Holds her hand, strokes her arm.*]

ELAINE : Please Mr Porter.

GEORGE : Uh-uh — Georgie.

ELAINE : Please Georgie —

GEORGE : [*Encouraged as before.*] We *are* getting familiar.

ELAINE : [*Resisting.*] I thought Harry was bad enough.
GEORGE : Don't call him Harry — makes me jealous. [*Getting ardent.*]
ELAINE : Do you mind?
GEORGE : Elaine — let's run Australia together — [*She starts around the desk again. He pursues her.*] or let's just run — [*They circle desk as before. Enter* ERWIN, *who falls in behind, so that all three are circling.*]
ERWIN : Highness! Excellence! The American ambassador becomes importunate!
GEORGE : [*Slowing to a halt.*] Phew. You'll really have to stop reading those books —
ERWIN : Mr Floyd P. Supple paces the hall!
GEORGE : I warn you Erwin! I'll dress you in doublet and hose! Show him in, show him in.
   [ELAINE *starts to sneak off. She's nearly there when* GEORGE,*with a sudden spasm of discomfort, clasps his backside and runs towards her.*]
ELAINE : Stop chasing me! I'm resigning!
GEORGE : It's not you! There's so much roughage moving through me I feel like a wheat silo! [*They exit. Enter* SUPPLE. *He notes empty office, produces cigar and lighter, puts former in mouth, waves latter over documents on desk, obviously photographing. Re-enter* GEORGE, *to flushing noises.* SUPPLE *recovers.*]
SUPPLE : Cigar?
GEORGE : Thanks
SUPPLE : [*Trying to light it for him.*] Damn things never work. [*Impatiently.*] Norman —
GEORGE : George. The name is George. And tell your president that too.
SUPPLE : George — let's get right down to thumbtacks.
GEORGE : Tintacks. If we're getting down to anything, it's tintacks. That's what they're called in this country Floyd. Sidewalks, elevators, automobiles, working breakfasts — you people have been getting your way for too long.
SUPPLE : I have just received a personal message from the president of the United States — the Soviet Union has complete details of our embargo plans for Mujik — Japanese electronics, Australian wool, the lot. Where'd they get those

details? From you Mr Porter. From your country. Mr Percha.

GEORGE: I unmasked the man — what more do you want?

SUPPLE: After he'd photographed the documents on this desk! You people don't know the first damn thing about security!

GEORGE: That's not going to happen any more. No one gets to the documents on my desk — no one. Go over to that cupboard, Mr Supple.

SUPPLE: Is that necessary Mr Porter?

GEORGE: Go over — open it — what do you see?

SUPPLE: A squash racquet with a bent frame —

GEORGE: What else?

SUPPLE: [*Producing a new broom, puzzled.*] That's the only other damn thing in here — a broom.

GEORGE: A new broom, Mr Supple — you follow me? New leadership. New policies. Did I hear you say embargo plans for Australian wool?

SUPPLE: Your predecessor, Mr Shanahan, gave us an undertaking —

GEORGE: It's not my plan Mr Supple. I haven't got a plan.

SUPPLE: The president wants you to act fast — teach the Mujiks a lesson.

GEORGE: Maybe so and maybe not. I'll have to think about it.

SUPPLE: The wool lobby — that's what you're scared of — offending the wool lobby — losing the numbers.

GEORGE: That's none of your business.

SUPPLE: No? Well, get this. We're about to lift our import quotas on your goddamned awful hamburger meat. If you don't embargo your Mujik wool, we won't take your meat. Then you'll have the cattle lobby on top of you. And a bull weighs more than a sheep.

GEORGE: Are you blackmailing me Supple?

SUPPLE: I'm telling you the facts about your damn fool, insignificant, down-under, she'll-be-right, fill-'em-up-again, see-yer-later, 'ow-ya-goin', waltzing-matilda, up-there-Cazaly little country. You need us more than we need you.

GEORGE: I don't need you Supple. Not a moment longer.

SUPPLE: I'm going — and so are you. Enjoy it up there on your high horse. You won't be there long. [*Starts to leave.*]

GEORGE: [*Getting up and going for him, only to be stopped at*

the last minute by ERWIN, *who rushes in just in time.*] Get going — before I give you one in the credentials!
ERWIN: [*Putting his head down and banging his fists on the desk in despair.*] *Mein Gott! Gotterdammerung!* No one talks like that to America!

[*Blackout.*]

SCENE 9

Darkness. The Porters' bedroom. GEORGE *is having a nightmare.*

GEORGE: Harry! I'm sorry! We'll play it again! Please Harry! Please! [*Lamp goes on.* BARBARA *and* GEORGE *are in bed. By now, he is out of it.*]
BARBARA: What's the matter with you? For God's sake!
GEORGE: I was on a squash court with Harry. We were playing in the dark. He was — luminous. We—he —
BARBARA: Control yourself!
GEORGE: For some reason he was formally dressed — he wore shorts, with a black jacket with all his decorations — I could hear them clinking and rattling as he ran round the court.
BARBARA: Go back to sleep.
GEORGE: I can't sleep! Problems, pressures . . . that bloody American envoy's infiltrating my cabinet — he's telling everybody I'm wrecking the Australian/American alliance . . . you know what the Yanks mean by an alliance — them on top and us underneath — the missionary position — I've had enough of that posture . . . Australian/American subservience — that's what we ought to call it . . . well to hell with it . . . I've got the wool lobby — but he's corraling up the cattle lobby against me.
BARBARA: Go back to sleep.
GEORGE: What am I going to do? Be hanged for a sheep or a bull? [*Pause.*] Harry wore this strange red cummerbund from his shoulder to his waist — blood red, as if he'd been slashed across the body —
BARBARA: You'll have to pull yourself together. You've got what you always wanted —

GEORGE : Over his dead body.

BARBARA : It was an accident.

GEORGE : I lost control — I killed him ... he attacked me, I fought back, then kept on going ... "I'm sorry George." That's the last thing he said. We went on bikerides together — we went yabbying when Glen Waverley *was* a glen — all bushland and orchards. Magpies swooped from the pinetrees, pecking at our heads — I should never have gone into politics!

BARBARA : After all these years, when you finally make it to the top — you don't *deserve* to be prime minister.

GEORGE : I probably won't be very much longer. A few scrubbers are gathering around Black Jack McConnell. By next week it could be a herd. Then a stampede. The beef boys'll trample us to death.

[*He puts light out. She puts it on again.*]

BARBARA : You've given in!

GEORGE : You can't fight America!

BARBARA : If you can't fight it, go and see it. Go see the president.

GEORGE : I don't want to see the president. His envoy is bad enough.

BARBARA : Pay him a visit. Shake his hand. Explain your problem to him. Talk it over. Man to man.

GEORGE : Protocols, rigmaroles, brass bands, red carpets — I hate it.

BARBARA : Pay him a flying visit. Your stocks are low. You've done nothing about inflation or unemployment. The tents are still out there on Capitol Hill. And you've alienated America. If you go see him, you can mend the breach, and look like a statesman. Persuade him to give up the wool embargo. Make him an offer.

GEORGE : I've got nothing to offer. And I wouldn't offer it to them even if I did! I don't like America. Their snap-frozen, takeaway, micro-wave, drip-dry, magi-mix, barbi-doll, siliconchip, drive-in, six-gun, coca-cola, hi-ya-baby lifestyle! It's a poison! Keep it out!

BARBARA : That's irrelevant! You can use him — like he's using you. Come on. [*Picks up phone.*] The bold stroke! Ring him direct. He's probably just in from his jogging. You can be there in forty-eight hours! Confound your enemies and do it!

GEORGE : No!
BARBARA : Okay then, I'll ring him. [*Consulting little book.*] I know the combination —
GEORGE : You're not doing it!
BARBARA : I am doing it! Your position's at stake!
GEORGE : Okay damn you! I'll do it!
[*Goes to phone. Pauses. Lights down, as he dials.*]

SCENE 10

GEORGE *and* BARBARA, *with overnight bags, wait before the doors that now represent the entrance to the U.S.* PRESIDENT's *office. On other side of stage sits* MR OMIRA, *prime minister of Japan. He is in a lounge suit,* GEORGE *in more formal attire.*

GEORGE : [*Yanking at his stiff collar.*] This is ridiculous! It's supposed to be an informal visit! No one dresses like this at 8.30 in the morning! Especially when they've spent all night in a damned plane.
BARBARA : [*Preoccupied with a magazine.*] It's called a morning suit, stupid . . . it's like a dentist's waiting room, right down to the back numbers of the *Reader's Digest* . . . "It pays to increase your word power" . . . "My most unforgettable character" . . . "Hysterectomy without hysteria".
GORGE : Wait on — isn't that Omira over there?
BARBARA : Omira? That's an Irish name.
GEORGE : Quite possibly — they'd copy anything . . . it *is* Omira — the prime minister of Japan! He's waiting to see the president too — in a lounge suit! [*He starts to undress.*]
BARBARA : [*Pulling lounge suit out of bag.*] Don't want to make a diplomatic gaffe — you will though, I know it.
GEORGE : [*Changing frantically.*] Wait a minute — he's supposed to be putting an embargo on Mujik too — cutting off their electronic equipment.
BARBARA : [*Turning, as if looking out window.*] Oh look — I think I can see him — it's him.
GEORGE : [*Ignoring her and watching* OMIRA *carefully.*] He's here for the same reason I am — bet you any money you like. He's got an electronics lobby like I've got a wool lobby.

BARBARA: I can see the president — he's jogging over the White House lawns —

GEORGE: It's going to be neck and neck — whoever gets his ear first — jogging? Did you say jogging?

BARBARA: In his shorts — quickly — [*Producing shorts etc. from bag.*]

GEORGE: [*Again changing, even more rapidly.*] Jesus, this is ridiculous.

BARBARA: Hurry up — he's coming this way — little skinny man with white legs with huge secret servicemen all round him. [*A moment after* GEORGE *starts to change,* OMIRA *does likewise.* GEORGE *is slightly ahead, so that when the* PRESIDENT *jogs onto the stage, puffing and blowing, he is able to give chase first.* OMIRA *does likewise, but is hampered by being only half-dressed.*]

GEORGE: Mr President!

OMIRA: Mister Plesident!
[*They get in each other's way and fall in a heap.* PRESIDENT *jogs offstage.*]

BARBARA: You fool, you've missed him.

GEORGE: [*Extricating himself.*] Excuse me. What time was your appointment?

OMIRA: Thirty of the minutes past the eight.

GEORGE: Eight thirty? That's the time of my appointment.

OMIRA: I am extremely of the apologies about that.

GEORGE: So am I pal, so am I. You're talking to the prime minister of Australia. I'm afraid I'll have to go first.

OMIRA: Aha — you afraid. I'm not afraid to go first. To see president, big nation come before small nation.

BARBARA: [*Watching at window.*] He's turning! He's doing another lap!

GEORGE: Confucius say — big prime minister of little country comes before little prime minister of big country.

OMIRA: [*Readying himself for karate.*] Insult to refer to physique in delogatory fashion!

GEORGE: Come on — stretch up and give us one on the knee.
[GEORGE *takes chop and goes down.* OMIRA *gets in behind the* PRESIDENT *as he jogs on stage again.*]

BARBARA: [*Helping him up.*] It's all in the footwork George. All you do is put yours in your mouth.

GEORGE : That's the last iron ore they get from us.
[PRESIDENT *pauses, puffing, jogging on the spot, then does some knee bends and perhaps pressups.* OMIRA *whispers to him confidentially, imitating whatever exercise the* PRESIDENT *is doing.* PRESIDENT *is nodding his head, as if* OMIRA *is getting a sympathetic hearing.*]
BARBARA : Get in there and pitch! The electric koala, quickly!
[*She produces it. He jogs over to* PRESIDENT *with it.*]
GEORGE : [*Pushing* OMIRA *aside.*] Mr President: George F. Porter, of Australia. Allow me to present you with this enchanting toy koala. Embedded within it is an ultra modern transistor, that, when you press its little eye, plays our national song. [*He presses. Silence.*]
OMIRA : Your technology is a laughter! Is twenty years backside!
GEORGE : What the hell are you talking about. [*Shaking koala.*]
OMIRA : You are twenty years backside! Bottom! Buttock!
BARBARA : Behind! He means we're twenty years behind!
GEORGE : Yair? [*Turning koala over.*] Get this.
OMIRA : [*Stunned.*] Is made in Japan?
GEORGE : [*Seizing his opportunity.*] Mr President — Australia — remember? Down Under? Fuzzy-wuzzy Angels? Moresby? Midway? MacArthur? I shall return? Aussies and Yanks, in it together! There he goes, wading through the water — or is he walking on it?
BARBARA : [*From the sidelines, clapping.*] Good on you George.
PRESIDENT : [*Stopping his exercises.*] We were together then, and we're together now — [*Shadow boxing.*] We'll teach those Mujiks a lesson. No wheat from us, no timber from Canada, no machinery from England, and no wool from you. We'll embargo 'em back to the Stone Age.
GEORGE : And no electronics from Japan? No electronics?
[PRESIDENT *looks straight ahead.* OMIRA *leaves, trying to conceal the fact that he has won a favour.*]
GEORGE : You've let him off! Haven't you?
BARBARA : [*From sidelines.*] George — George —
GEORGE : Your old wartime ally. Thanks very much. Never mind about the Kokoda Trail and Tarakan and Salamaua. If they're not going to embargo, we're not either. One in, all in.
PRESIDENT : I don't want that wool to go.
GEORGE : I'll decide that.
PRESIDENT : I'm telling you right now. No wool. Let 'em freeze.

GEORGE : And I'm telling you that wool is going. I've just made up my mind.

PRESIDENT : It ain't going . . . hamburger meat . . . remember?

GEORGE : Don't treat us like a banana republic. It is going.

PRESIDENT : It ain't. [*Throwing koala at* GEORGE.]

GEORGE : [*Throwing it back.*] It is!

PRESIDENT : It — [*Kicking it like a football.*] ain't! [*As it lands "Waltzing Matilda" strikes up.* GEORGE *tears down American flag and jumps on it.*]

GEORGE : It — is!

[*Thunder sounds.* PRESIDENT *points accusingly at* GEORGE. *Freeze. Darkness.*]

SCENE 11

ERWIN, *pacing up and down before the prime ministerial doors, reading, finally aloud —*

ERWIN : "Indeed, what compels us to assume there exists any essential antithesis between true and false? Is it not enough to suppose grades of apparentness and as it were lighter and darker shades and tones of appearance — different valeurs, to speak the language of the painters?" [*He breaks off, hearing voices. Enter* GEORGE *and* BARBARA, *with bags. During the ensuing dialogue,* ERWIN *tries to catch his master's attention, but seeing his mood, never quite summons the courage.*]

GEORGE : Damned Yank. Who does he think he is.

BARBARA : The president of the United States, that's who he is.

GEORGE : And I'm the prime minister of Australia.

BARBARA : Not for much longer after that little performance. Wait till that gets back. Ah well, back to the Tai Chi.

ERWIN : Sir! Sir!

GEORGE : Shut up Erwin . . . we're going to have a bit of leadership for a change. We're not going to kiss America's arse any more. And that's spelt a-r-s-e not a-s-s.

ERWIN : Sir! Sir!

GEORGE : [*Taking it out on him.*] And we're going to kick yours more often.

BARBARA : [*Ironically.*] Great. What a slogan. You'll win 'em with that one.

GEORGE : [*Defiant.*] I'll campaign in front of a bare bum: We're not going to kiss it anymore!

BARBARA : [*Taking bags off.*] Might as well leave 'em packed. We'll be leaving The Lodge anyway.

GEORGE : [*After her.*] It was your idea I go over.

BARBARA : [*Back at him.*] Yes — and you went over really well.

ERWIN : Sir! Sir! An attack from the flank!

[*He presses switch. Doors open. Music.* BLACK JACK McCON-NELL *sits at* GEORGE's *desk.*]

GEORGE : Black Jack McConnell of the beef lobby! What are you doing at my desk?

BLACK JACK : I'm staying here, that's what I'm doing. Till we can find someone with a bit of common sense to run the country. You can't talk to the president of the United States like that.

GEORGE : That's the problem. No one *has* talked to the president of the United States like that. I didn't take any nonsense from him, and I'm not taking any from you either. Erwin, throw this man out.

[ERWIN *moves towards him, a strange combination of the aggressive and the servile.*]

BLACK JACK : Mr Gruber, open that side door!

[ERWIN *instinctively moves to obey, torn between two masters.*]

GEORGE : Erwin, out with him!

BLACK JACK : Open that side door when you're told! —

[ERWIN, *cringing, whining, dog-like, rushes back and forth, trapped between his orders.*]

BLACK JACK : For the Grand Old Man of the Party!

[*This name is too much for* ERWIN. *He succumbs.*]

ERWIN : [*Going to get him, mumbling.*] The Grand Old Man of the Party! The Grand Old Man of the Party!

[ERWIN *reappears, wheeling* THE GRAND OLD MAN *in a wheelchair, bowing obeisances to him as he does so.*]

GEORGE : [*Defiantly.*] He's asleep!

BLACK JACK : [*In his ear, respectfully.*] Grand Old Man! Grand Old Man!

GRAND OLD MAN : [*Stirring.*] "In Clause 3, Page 3, Line 3, insert the following —"

BLACK JACK: There's your enemy Grand Old Man! There's your Judas!

GRAND OLD MAN: I spent years building the American alliance! [*Wheeling at* GEORGE, *swishing stick.*] What I have joined together, let no man put asunder.

GEORGE: We're not a banana republic any more! [*Avoiding his lunges.*] We grow our own!

GRAND OLD MAN: Ten million whites — in an Asian sea! [*Wheeling.*]

GEORGE: [*Avoiding.*] Fifteen million, Grand Old Man. That's enough feet to stand on!

GRAND OLD MAN: Without powerful friends, we'll be invaded!

GEORGE: We've been invaded — by the powerful friend! Captain Marvel, Colonel Sanders and General Motors.

BLACK JACK: To the Labor Party, where you belong!

GEORGE: I'm for the little man!

GRAND OLD MAN: Because you *are* a little man. Get him out! Of the job! Of the party!

GEORGE: You'll never get the numbers.

BLACK JACK: I've got the numbers and I've called a party meeting! You've got thirty minutes to live! [*Wheels* GRAND OLD MAN *off.*]

GEORGE: [*To* ERWIN, *who's been fawning upon and assisting them.*] Stop your damned cringing and fawning.

ERWIN: [*Turning against him.*] Schweinhund!

GEORGE: Oh God, I'm finished. Elaine! Elaine!

ERWIN: Pig-dog!

GEORGE: Out! Go snuffling after your new masters.

ERWIN: [*Cuffing* GEORGE *as he scurries out.*] Gott in Himmel!

[*Pause.* GEORGE *sits at the desk with his head down. Enter* ELAINE.]

GEORGE: That damned little Kraut's deserting the ship — he called me a pig-dog and whacked me over the head. Don't you leave me. [*Holding her hand.*]

ELAINE: Please Mr Porter — [*Resisting.*]— what's happened?

GEORGE: I've alienated America. The unforgiveable sin. Let's commit it together.

ELAINE: Please Mr Porter!

GEORGE: Georgie! Isn't anyone going to be my friend?

ELAINE: Please Georgie!

GEORGE : [*Making more advances.*] We *are* getting familiar.
[*Enter* BARBARA, *who wrongfully assumes* ELAINE *to be the seductress.*]
BARBARA : Get up! At once!
ELAINE : That's it. That's the finish. Get someone else to fend him off. "Wanted — secretary — middle distance running skills an advantage." [*Exits.*]
BARBARA : What a tartar! Your next one will be six axehandles across, I'll see to that.
GEORGE : There won't be a next one. At this very moment, pins are being stuck into my effigy in the party room.
BARBARA : You fool — I warned you.
GEORGE : They're voting me out at an extraordinary meeting of the party.
BARBARA : And you just sit here fondling your secretary? The phone, quickly! Activate the cameras . . . wake the press officer from his torpor . . . justify yourself — to the nation!
[*She gives instructions over phone.*]
GEORGE : What's the use? Australians don't *want* to be independent. They've sniffed, smoked, seen and swallowed America for so long they can't do without it.
BARBARA : Present your case — while there's still time.
GEORGE : It's hopeless!
BARBARA : A week in power — and you've blown it.
GEORGE : I've done the undoable. The unforgiveable. Alienated America!
BARBARA : Get to those cameras — before Black Jack McConnell does.
[*TV light up on camera, chair, table, at side of stage. Enter* DIRECTOR/CAMERAMAN *and* ERWIN, *who both start fussing. As* ERWIN *fusses, he mutters to himself, saying some of the words out loud, causing the* DIRECTOR *to look up in surprise. This is concurrent with what is going on with* GEORGE *and* BARBARA.]
ERWIN : [*Muttering, fussing, chuckling to himself.*] "Men not high or hard enough for the artistic refashioning of mankind; men not strong enough to allow the law of failure and death to prevail . . ."
GEORGE : [*Still with* BARBARA.] It's a plot. Their damned ambassador warned me what would happen if I stood up to them.

BARBARA : Quick — tell them there's been a plot! Accuse the ambassador — get people's sympathy — [*She's pushing him towards the TV lights. As he emerges into them,* BLACK JACK *does also from the other side.*]

GEORGE : I — have an important announcement.

BLACK JACK : So have I. I'm the new leader. I'm sending you to Mujik. You'll be popular over there.

GEORGE : [*Trying to get into chair in front of camera.*] The people, I must tell the people! [*They wrestle, both trying to get into the chair.*] It's an American plot! The ambassador's behind it! I'm telling the people!

[*An imbroglio follows involving* BLACK JACK, GEORGE, TV DIRECTOR, BARBARA *and* ERWIN, *in which the following snatches of dialogue emerge, as the group move in and out of the TV lights.*]

ERWIN : [*Striking* GEORGE.] Schwein! Pig dog!

BARBARA : [*Striking* ERWIN.] Two-timing little Kraut!

BLACK JACK : [*Finally.*] Police! Take him away!

[*Enter* POLICEMAN.]

GEORGE : I am the prime minister — take him away!

BLACK JACK : I am the new prime minister — take *him* away!

[GEORGE *is taken into the darkness, struggling and expostulating. Meanwhile* BLACK JACK *brushes himself down, smooths his hair, confers with* DIRECTOR. *Brighter light. Cue from* DIRECTOR. *Action.*]

BLACK JACK : [*Still slightly breathlessly.*] Good afternoon — or is it evening? There is an old Flemish proverb that goes something like this: "the world is a haystack and every man plucks from it what he can". I am appearing before you at this moment with the intention of making a special announcement. I am your new prime minister. It may seem unusual that I am the third such person to lay claim to this title within a matter of weeks. However, when one considers the pressures that go with the position, it will come as no surprise to you to learn that Mr George Porter has been compelled, under doctor's orders, to stand down. My name is Sir John McConnell and I hope we will be together a long time —

[*He pauses, there being a disturbance upstage.* GEORGE *has broken free, run back through the office doors to his desk, pressed a switch, and as the doors close, yells out —*]

GEORGE : *I* am your prime minister!

BLACK JACK : [*With* DIRECTOR *signalling him to stop.*] I will be back with you in a moment after this short commercial message . . . [*Gets up.*] What on earth is going on?

ERWIN : Swine! He's locked himself in his office.

BLACK JACK : [*Cuffing him.*] *My* office! Get him out!

ERWIN : He has the key in his desk!

BLACK JACK : [*Cuffing him again.*] *My* desk! I've got one too.

GEORGE : [*Voice only, over P/A system.*] Can you hear me out there? I'm putting our armed forces on red alert! I'm ringing the president of the U.S. on the hot line — I'm dialling! [*After frantic unlocking, the doors part.* GEORGE *is on the phone.*]

GEORGE : President? It's Porter. If you hear a snapping sound, it's because we're breaking off diplomatic relations — [BLACK JACK *hits him with the squash racquet, while* ERWIN *says something in German into phone then hangs up. Lights and sounds swirl, suggesting a sinking into unconsciousness.*]

SCENE 12

GEORGE *is in bed, asleep. Enter* BARBARA.

BARBARA : George . . . George . . . snap out of it George.

GEORGE : [*Coming to, mumbling.*] I'm sorry Harry . . . accidental Harry, I swear it . . . go on, hit me Harry . . .

BARBARA : Stop it!

GEORGE : [*He wakes. Sits up. Suddenly alert.*] The despatch boxes, quickly!

BARBARA : It's all over George. You're not prime minister any more.

GEORGE : [*Reciting.*]
"Caesar should be a beast without a heart
if he should stay at home today for fear —
No — [*Getting out of bed.*]— Caesar shall not."
[*He totters, and is assisted back to bed.*] As a boy, at school, I had to learn large slabs of *Julius Caesar.*

BARBARA : You're not well George. I've brought someone along to see you.

[*She beckons.* Enter SYNDROME, *whom* GEORGE *addresses—*]

GEORGE: "Stoop Romans stoop
And let us bathe our hands in Caesar's blood
Up to the elbows."

BARBARA: George, this is Mr Syndrome . . . he can help you.

GEORGE: [*Accusingly.*]
"A curse shall light upon the limbs of men
Domestic fury and fierce civil strife
Shall cumber all the parts of Italy."

SYNDROME: [*Waving* BARBARA *out.*] Mr Porter? I wonder if I could ask you a few simple questions.

GEORGE: Call me George . . . Georgie . . . let's run Australia together . . . that's what I said to her . . .

SYNDROME: Wild animals . . .

GEORGE: Eh?

SYNDROME: Are you nervous of them even when they're in cages?

GEORGE: Eh?

SYNDROME: Your hands.

GEORGE: Eh?

SYNDROME: Do you make a point of washing them before meals?

GEORGE: Eh?

SYNDROME: Your looks.

GEORGE: Eh?

SYNDROME: Do you worry about your looks?

GEORGE: I know who you are! The American ambassador! [*Trying to wrench off his beard.*] That beard is false! You're masters of technology!

SYNDROME: [*In desperation.*] Mr Porter —

GEORGE: George — Georgie . . .

SYNDROME: George — Georgie — I want to help you.

GEORGE: Help me? To do what?

SYNDROME: You think you're prime minister of Australia.

GEORGE: I *am* prime minister of Australia.

SYNDROME: You *were* prime minister of Australia.

GEORGE: I'm the victim of a plot organized by the Americans. Listen to me. The CIA did it. I am the legitimate, elected, leader of this country. Tell the world. Release it to the papers. I am being held here in a drugged condition against my will. Think of it — the prime minister — stripped of his powers and held incommunicado!

SYNDROME : Mr Porter, which of the following is not a make of car? Rofd, Ragnudov, Teylene, Metoc, Taif.

GEORGE : Eh?

SYNDROME : They're jumbled. The letters are mixed up. Which of the following is not a famous poet? Steak, Yornb, Crehuca, Ranibas.

GEORGE : Eh?

SYNDROME : Of the next four jumbled words, one is not a famous composer. Zotram, Satsurs, Revid, Maleso.

GEORGE : If Zotram's a famous composer, I'm a jew's harp. Are you bonkers?

SNDROME : Nithgorb, Dolnon, Poorlivel, Sowlgag, Reexet. Which of these towns is not in England?

GEORGE : Sowlgag? Nithgorb? One of us is mad, I'm sure of it.

SYNDROME : [*Unfolding large ink-blot.*] What does this shape suggest to you?

GEORGE : Antarctica. Either that — or a bishop fornicating with a buffalo.

SYNDROME : Aha! Super ego and id! Conscience at war with instinct. An opening at last! In we go. Chair, stool, leg, anus. Link them in pairs.

GEORGE : Chair and leg. Stool and anus.

SYNDROME : How on earth do you explain that?

GEORGE : The leg comes out of the chair and the stool comes out of the anus.

SYNDROME : Aha! Fantasies of orgasmic incontinence in relation to seductive faecal objects! He's sublimating the repression caused by this conflict into a longing for control over the outside world. He sees all Australia as an uncontrolled bowel.

GEORGE : Crap!

SYNDROME : Exactly! You both crave and despise authority — hence your attitude to America. You want a father figure — but only so you can reject him! — Mrs Porter, we can save this man! [*Exits.*]

GEORGE : [*Getting out of bed.*] All I want to do is make this wonderful country of ours a better place to live in . . .

[*He exits. Enter* SYNDROME *and* BARBARA, *who say, in unison . . .*]

BARBARA, SYNDROME : He's gone!

[*Blackout.*]

SCENE 13

NORMA *and* IAN CITIZEN *sit listlessly watching TV*

IAN : Jesus, not again. [*Getting up to change channels.*] Another swearing in. It's Black Jack McConnell! That's the second in two weeks.

NORMA : Hang on, I want to watch it.

IAN : Look at those beady eyes. Like a ferret coming up for air. I want to watch Starsky and Hutch. [*Turns it over.*]

NORMA : Turn it back Ian.

IAN : We always watch Starsky and Hutch at eight o'clock. [*Turns it back.*]

NORMA : Hang on, he's praising George Porter.

IAN : Jesus, that won't take long.

NORMA : Very sick man, apparently. Gone somewhere quiet to rest.

IAN : Rest? He was only in the job a week . . . we've missed five minutes of Starsky and Hutch.

NORMA : Look at Black Jack. Got a face like a football. As if it's been pumped up . . . Ian, what's that noise?

IAN : It's you talking. That's the only noise I can hear.

NORMA : Ian — there's someone — getting in the window — Ian! [*Enter* GEORGE, *dishevelled.*]

IAN : Hey! What's going on? Get out of here!

GEORGE : Don't be alarmed. I'm George Porter.

IAN : Yair? And I'm Black Jack McConnell. Go on, get! Quick!

NORMA : [*To* IAN. Keep him talking — I'll ring the police. [*Exits.*]

IAN : You're George Porter are you? Looking like that?

GEORGE : I've been in hiding — [*Taking some potato crisps.*] may I? I'm starving — they're trying to get me.

IAN : Oh they are, are they? Who are?

GEORGE : [*Pointing to TV.*] He is, that's who. Him. Look at him, holding the bible with his arm up in the air as if margarine wouldn't melt in his mouth — [*To TV.*] — No! Interloper! *I* am the real prime minister of this country! The Yanks got you in, not the people! [IAN *turns it over.*] Don't do that! I was watching that!

IAN : I'm sorry — I know I've got a bit of a cheek, but *I* want to watch Starsky and Hutch.

GEORGE : Poison — from America! It's everywhere. Listen — the Americans tried to blackmail me, don't you understand? Embargo your wool to Mujik — or we won't take your hamburger meat. I defied them — and look where I am.
[*A knock at the door.*] Hide me! [*He hides. Enter* NORMA *and* POLICEMAN. *Silently* IAN *indicates where he is.*]

POLICEMAN : Come on, come on —

GEORGE : I hope you realize what you've done. You have just passed up the last chance you had to stop — the invasion! They saved us from the Japanese — so they could take us over slowly. They don't storm the beaches — they infiltrate the TV channels like carp — eating every native fish they can find ... [*He is taken away.*] Go on. Drink it in. The carp are coming. Let the commercials nibble away at you! Nibble nibble! One night, after the ten thousandth advertisement, there'll be nothing left! Just a beer can and a cigarette butt! Nibble nibble nibble nibble! [*His voice fades away as he goes.*]

IAN : [*Going over and turning TV sound up.*] Trust that to happen! Right in the middle of my favourite bloody programme.
[*He starts watching.*]

NORMA : Poor chap's off his head ... it's the unemployment. The strain of it drives them to it ... you'll have to see about that window ... any Tom, Dick and Harry can get in —

IAN : [*Shaking his head in desperation and turning sound up again so that it is deafening.*] Quiet!

NORMA : It's too loud. Turn it down! [*It seems to get even louder.*]

IAN : I can't! I'm trying —

NORMA : Turn it down! It's killing me!

IAN : Something's happened to the volume knob! I can't!
[*Lights slowly down. They put their heads in their hands to escape from the din. Then crouch on the floor, as if they're overcome by it. Darkness.*]

Other Plays Published by University of Queensland Press

Three Australian Plays edited by Eunice Hanger (formerly *Khaki, Bush, and Bigotry*)
  Rusty Bugles by Sumner Locke Elliott
  We Find the Bunyip by Ray Mathew
  The Well by Jack McKinney

6 One-act Plays edited by Eunice Hanger
  The Spiders by Ron Hamilton
  I've Come About the Assassination by Tony Morphett
  Witzenhausen, Where Are You? by Barry Oakley
  A Squeaking of Rats by Elizabeth Perkins
  The Man on the Mountain by Irene M. Summy
  The Pier by Michael Thomas

4 Australian Plays by Barbara Stellmach
  Dark Heritage
  Dust in the Heart
  Hang Your Clothes on Yonder Bush
  Legend of the Losers

Mischief in the Air: Radio and Stage Plays by Max Afford
  Consulting Room
  Lazy in the Sun
  Awake My Love
  Lady in Danger
  Mischief in the Air

Melba by Paul Sherman

Five Plays for Stage, Radio, and Television edited by Alrene Sykes
  The Drovers by Louis Esson
  The One Day of the Year by Alan Seymour
  What If You Died Tomorrow by David Williamson
  The Golden Lover by Douglas Stewart
  Lindsay's Boy by Ted Roberts

2D and Other Plays by Eunice Hanger
  2D
  The Frogs
  Flood